My Journey of Taekwondo:

From Korea to America

Master Jung K. Lee

Also by Master Jung K. Lee:

The Science of Tae Kwon Do

태권도의과학 *(in Korean)*

굼벵이사범의 좌충우돌 미국체험기 *(in Korean)*

My Journey of Taekwondo:

From Korea to America

Master Jung K. Lee

We want to hear from you. Please send your comments about this book to us in care of masterjunglee@gmail.com.

Thank you.

My Journey of Taekwondo:

From Korea to America

Copyright © 2019 by Master Jung K. Lee

This book is dedicated

to the martial arts ancestors

and

to the hundreds of martial arts families

in the world.

CONTENTS

ACKNOWLEDGMENTS

I wish to thank my immediate and extended family for their energies and guidance in helping to bring this project to completion. I further wish to express my gratitude to all my martial arts associates, partners, and colleagues for their support, brotherhood, and sisterhood along this amazing journey.

And to everyone around the world
who believes in the infinite potential of life and spirit.

Prologue

Whether we like it or not, we each have a path to follow. That is life. With no guidance, I walked down my path with only a backpack on my back. On my journey, I experienced many hardships and failures, and I have yet to reach the threshold of success. I have settled here in America after much physical labor and many misunderstandings.

During my struggles, I wished to hear about their life experiences. How invaluable would it have been to me to learn from the lives that they had led, whether they experienced success or failure? How much could a backpack-clad youth like me have gained from reading such real-life tales? I had no such opportunity when I came to America. Forget success stories of Taekwondo Masters! I just hoped to hear mundane stories about the regular lives of someone who had already experienced America, to get even a little glimpse of the American life that would, I hoped, come to me. I combed through Taekwondo publications, but it was difficult to find any books written about those kinds of daily experiences. Stories about accomplishment are certainly essential for people beginning their lives in America, but I felt stories of the ordinary folk like me, who limped his way through failures, might be useful as well. I can only offer a story of a life full of trials and errors, but perhaps it can be a roadmap for avoiding unnecessary hardships.

I believe that what our seniors have experienced, what we are experiencing right this moment, and the lessons of life within these experiences together form a pearl. This pearl is the actual history, philosophy, and spirit of Taekwondo. Therefore, when all our experiences, successful or not, are collected and recorded, the necessary nutrients for the pearl of Taekwondo to grow will be produced. If we thoroughly research these accumulated pieces of knowledge, I believe we will also obtain the wisdom to overcome easily the many problems we face today.

It burdens my heart to put out an unimportant man's story when there isn't even enough time to read and follow the lives of great, successful people. However, I take courage in the hope that I may inspire others to share the stories buried in their own hearts. Here, I write about bits and pieces of the common life of a man. I hope you find my vignettes helpful and use them as stepping stones to tread lightly across the muddy world.

Respectfully,

Master Jung K. Lee

Chapter 1: A Dreaming Worm

In Korea, I lived as though tied on a leash, going back and forth mindlessly from school to home to the dojang (Taekwondo studio). I have no memories of going on a trip, something considered to be a privilege of youth. I wasn't really a good student; I was never in much of a mindset to pursue challenges. My desire to experience a wider world was just a vague, uninformed yearning, like that of a worm stuck in a cave dreaming of a wider world. When I crossed the Pacific, I did it without a plan in my mind. So, of course, it was no surprise that I was easily kicked around. The misadventures of my youth began with one big problem.

English Was the Problem

Although a little different now, a high wall existed between English and me during school days. In my freshman year of university, I took English for my liberal arts class requirements. It was scheduled so that we took it together with another department in which there were a lot of female students. I was quite happy in the class because there were a lot of pretty girls! My mind was definitely not on the English lessons.

On the midterm exam, there was a short-answer question. You just had to read the explanatory text and answer in one word. I combined a few words that I knew as if reading a Chinese newspaper. The question that I got was: "Desert + Trade + Animal =?" I immediately thought of 'Nackta (camel in Korean).' I confidently wrote the answer and left. I checked with my friends. "It was 'Nackta' right?" Everyone said that was the answer. How long had it been since I got a short-answer question right? I was proud of myself.

The next class, the professor benignly asked the class, "Please raise your hand if you answered 'Nackta' in the short-answer question in last week's exam." I proudly raised my hand. But the atmosphere was not what I expected. Nobody had raised his or her hands but me. Everyone was looking at me. My heart sank with. Was I the only person to correctly answer such an easy question? That was an impossible assumption.

The professor asked, "Do you think that 'answer' is spelled 'N-a-c-k-t-a'?" That moment the class went crazy with laughter. Had I spelled it wrong? "Then should there be no 'k'?" And wouldn't you know, the class laughed even harder.

Tour Guide Interpreter

That summer, I left for vacation to the beach with my friends. I sneaked away wearing my older brother's pair of sunglasses and his cool red t-shirt with big white English words written across the chest. To me, whose hometown was inland, the seaside was a whole other world. Girls in swimsuits were swarming around. I didn't know how to swim though, so the sea and bath tub weren't that different to me. I splashed in the water a few times and then lay in the sand, watching the young ladies pass by through my sunglasses.

Then a white man with blond hair appeared in the distance. He was asking around for something, but it seemed no one understood what he was saying. I imagined how cool I would look if I could casually step in and interpret for him. The blond white man looked around with a troubled expression, and our eyes suddenly met. And wouldn't you know it, he started walking towards me with a smile! With my heart in my mouth, I turned my head away. 'Is he really coming towards me?' Out of the corner of my eye, I saw that he indeed was! This could not go well, so I quickly stood up and started to run away. I looked back after a few steps only to see him hurry his steps to catch up with me. 'Uh oh!' I walked faster. As my pace quickened, so did his. I was breathless from panic. I turned a corner, and, pretending to go to the bathroom, I ran into a crowded store. I peeked out from behind the shelves and saw the white man looking around with a confused expression, searching for me. It was only long after he had disappeared that I headed back to my spot, still looking around as I did so.

When my friends asked me where I had disappeared alone to, I answered truthfully that I was coming back from avoiding a white man who kept following me. "Do I look like I'm good at English?" At that all of them started rolling in the sand, clutching their stomachs with laughter. My friends teased me, "Are you stupid? How did you get into university?" The problem had been the red t-shirt that I had stolen from my older brother. It had "Tour Guide Interpreter" written in big white letters. My brother was a student majoring in tourism interpretation, and that t-shirt had been his department t-shirt!

Let's Learn English

Spooked by this incident, I signed up for an early morning English conversation course at the local academy. There was a team of 10 people in each class, and the lecturer would be speaking only in English during the class. (She wasn't a native speaker, but she had come back from a foreign language exchange.) First class, we introduced ourselves to each other in English and evaluated each person's level. I also answered as best as I could. I felt proud that I could hold my own with others in English. At the end of the lecture, the lecturer spoke about preparations for next class. From what I could gather, the class next day would be a free conversational class, and we would not be required to bring our textbooks. 'Yeah, I'm stronger at free conversation than studying with books!' Next daybreak, I arrived before anyone else to show my enthusiasm, positioned all the tables into a circle, and sat right next to the lecturer's seat. A little later, the students and the lecturer arrived. Once everyone had taken a seat, the lecturer gave the word, and all the students pulled out and opened their textbooks at once. I was the only one empty-handed. Everyone looked at me. 'Damn it, I was the only one to misunderstand again....' Discouraged, I quit the course that day.

Student-Athlete?

I had the opportunity to be the student body president of my college. That same year I was selected to be the state representative Taekwondo player in the national competition. Since I had to miss class during the national competition period, I went to the head of my department to ask for permission to be absent. I wore the representative player uniform, given by the state. My department head looked at me with puzzled eyes when I requested permission to be absent because of the national competition; I had only ever visited him previously to ask permission to be absent for reasons like overnight student orientations or college fairs. He asked me politely, "Does our department select student-athletes, too?" "Huh? Not to my knowledge, sir." "Then how is a student from our department participating in the Taekwondo national competition?"

I graduated with a degree in Physics. Nominally, I majored in Physics, but it was something I just picked up on the side during my four years at college. My specialty—if it can be called so—was Taekwondo, which I had been studying since I was a little boy. I spent much more time participating in Taekwondo demonstrations and competitions than studying my major. Consequently, I was considered a student-athlete in the physics department and treated as a physics student in the Taekwondo world. It was a life like a bat's going back and forth between two worlds, unable to be master in either.

Furthermore, people would tell me I look very different when I wore wearing my Taekwondo uniform than when I didn't. At a fall festival at our University, I asked my friends to help me with a demonstration. We successfully finished some crazy breaking demonstrations and were doing self-defense demonstrations, when one friend suggested making it more realistic and told me to hit him for real. I dodged his attack and kicked him with a roundhouse kick. My friend fell to the ground realistically. But then he didn't get up even when the demonstration ended. Seventh and eighth ribs fractured! At least, after this demonstration, the female students who looked down on me when they lent me their lecture notes would be impressed, or so I thought. When I changed out of my uniform, the student vice-president ran over to me. "Did you see? The guy who said he was from our department and did the Taekwondo demonstrations. Do you know who he is?" I was bewildered. "What? That was me." "Oh, stop joking around!" "It was really me!" "That's hilarious, you and Taekwondo. Don't be like that now, who was it?" No one believed me. In the end, I had just cracked my friend's ribs for nothing.

First Time in America, Little Tokyo Demonstration

Ever since I was young, my mother would say, "I'd like to see Gimpo International Airport once in my life because of you." (Inchon international airport was not built at that time.) Today, people freely travel overseas, but in the early 90s the Gimpo International Airport wasn't somewhere a hillbilly like me could casually stroll into. According to the TV Dramas I sometimes watched, it was a gate to a world that only successful people could come and go through.

A Taekwondo acquaintance had some business in Japan. I skipped lecture and followed him to Gimpo International Airport. If I think about it now, it was rather creepy of me. I made the excuse of seeing him off, but my real goal was to visit Gimpo International Airport. It was my first time seeing the airport and I was astounded. I determined that I would also fly out to the world through that gate someday!

In 1995, a chance to set foot onto American soil was given to me. The Taekwondo demonstration team that I was part of received an invitation to travel to Los Angeles, California. I took a night bus to Seoul and received my visa with difficulty after waiting in line in front of the American Embassy in Seoul from the crack of dawn. This country bumpkin was finally traveling overseas for the first time! America sounded all-around incredible.

After we were done with our demonstration schedule, we visited a famous Taekwondo school dojang located in Downtown Los Angeles. Seeing an action photo of their Grand Master reminded me of a movie poster I saw when I was little—The Ninja Turf. Their Grand Master, Grand Master Jun Chong, was the actor from the poster! I had stared at that poster intently as a youngster, because of the actor's handsome mustache and impressive action pose. Next to his action photo was a photo of Master Phillip Rhee! He was the main actor in the movie I was crazy about at the time, Best of the Best. Unfortunately, neither of them was present at the dojang that day.

While greeting the Master who was teaching class, we heard that a big demonstration competition would take place a few days later in the Japanese part of town, Little Tokyo. All kinds of Asian Martial Artists would be participating in it. I had seen Taekwondo and Aikido demonstrations in Korea, but in those days, it was a rare chance to be able to see martial arts from other countries. I was immediately intrigued, but the competition was to take place two days after our flight back to Korea. I made up my mind that I would stay and see it no matter what. I called Korean Air in private and pushed back my flight schedule to 4 days later. I told my Grand Master on the morning of the return flight that I would remain and return to Korea separately. Predictably, chaos ensued. "What? Young man, where do you think you are? Do you have money? Do you speak English?" I only had 50 dollars left in my wallet. And, of course, I didn't speak a word of English. But I reassured

12

him that I would somehow get by, and remained on my own. Once everyone had left, I took out the business cards I received from our demonstrations. After several calls, I was thankfully able to get a place to crash for sleep. And until the day of the demonstration competition, I just walked around on blistered feet throughout Los Angeles. When I was hungry, I would buy a bunch of bananas—the cheapest food I could find—to carry around and eat while still walking. The roads were wide open towards the horizon, but hardly anyone was walking around like me. Thinking back, I probably looked like I was homeless!

The day of the martial arts demonstration competition finally arrived, and I headed to Little Tokyo. The event was called Pan-Am Asian Martial Arts Festival. Arriving at the venue, I saw tents put up densely around the stage, each housing a different martial art. In addition to martial arts such as China's various Kung Fu teams and Japan's Jiujutsu, there were sword, spear, archery and other martial arts teams from South Asia that I had never seen before. Techniques I had never seen before, sharp sounds of yelling kihap, and excellent running and rolling moves. That day my eyes had the pleasure of feasting on them all.

Amongst all teams in the demonstration competition, there was only one Taekwondo team. It was not a casual environment. Each group would watch other teams carefully and critically. The atmosphere was such that if a team fell behind skill-wise, they would click their tongues, "tut, tut." Since the general atmosphere was like this, the Master of the Taekwondo team invited me to join their demonstration. There was no higher honor for me than to participate in a place like this. The level of this demonstration team of 8 people was substantial. Their dojang only allowed their students to receive 1st degree Black Belt after five years of training, and not to mention 2nd degree. So, their powerful, disciplined movements and clean skills had no flaws. I changed my uniform and was stretching with them when an elder Grand Master came over. He reprimanded the Master, because how could he let just anyone in at such an important competition? I was privately disappointed but said that I would step out if it was troublesome. However, the Master responsible for the demonstration team assured me that it was fine, and so I was able to participate after all. Finally, when it was our turn, everyone demonstrated their skills perfectly. Kicking while running, kicking with sequence, kicking and breaking boards—with such fast and strong kicks, no other martial art could follow Taekwondo

After some kicking demonstrations, I decided to finish with a fingertip thrust. The boards in America were thicker than in Korea. There were three remaining boards. I grabbed all of them on top of one another. The Master asked me if I was sure about this. But even if I ended up breaking my fingers, I couldn't back out. I told him not to worry. It was a little noisy, as the competition was outdoors, but when I screamed out my largest kihap possible and aimed my fingertips at the boards, there was a sudden silence. "No way." At that time, doing a spear finger thrust was not a common move in a demonstration. I took time for a good stance and struck the boards with my fingertips in one thrust. The boards broke in half with a large "crack" and my fingertips reached the chest of the assistant. The field was so quiet that I was embarrassed. 'Oh no, are they that unimpressed?' The silence went on for a moment, then suddenly cheers erupted. Even other martial arts team seemed to look at me in surprise, thinking, 'That guy!'

When I came down from the stage, the blonde MC lady ran towards me, asking if she could touch my hands. She fiddled with my hand with wonder. I took a photo with her and received very humbling hospitality. The elder Grand Master clapped me on the shoulders and told me, "Well done." After the demonstration, I walked around to explore tents of other martial arts and received glares. But I didn't feel offended at all. I was happy that they seemed to perceive me as someone who could stand by them as an equal opponent. Anyhow, that day became a valuable experience that broadened my narrow sight. The world is vast and martial art is endless!

Olympic Park Demonstration

The following year, another demonstration team formed in time for the 1996 Atlanta Olympics. At that time, it was complicated to get a United States visa, and a lot of people failed to receive theirs. Consequently, although unplanned, I had the chance to participate again. Perhaps the United States and I were meant to be. However, despite my high expectations, Atlanta wasn't as exciting as my first time in America. Unlike the exotic scenery of Western America, Atlanta, located in the eastern part of the country, wasn't that different from Korea climate-wise and landscape-wise. The Atlanta Olympics, later criticized as a failed Olympic event, did not even have a true Olympic atmosphere. The residents of Atlanta did not even know when the opening ceremony was. Apart from the downtown area where the main stadium and Olympic Park (in which cultural events were held) were located, I didn't detect a festive atmosphere. Furthermore, the Olympic Park was filled with heavily armed police forces to prevent terrorism, which dampened the merriment.

Our attempt to demonstrate in the streets of Olympic Park also failed due to the police. No group action was to be tolerated during the Olympics. A couple of cops followed us around in case we did a surprise demonstration. Their attitude told us they'd handcuff us if it came to it.

Just in time, a reporter from the national TV network ABC, saw us wearing our uniforms and asked us to perform an opening demonstration for the national live broadcast. When we told him, we couldn't because of the police, he turned to the police officers to persuade them. Later we found out that the reporter was someone quite famous. With his efforts, we were permitted to show one breaking technique in front of the camera. Finally, the cue sign came and the camera turned to us, showing "the live scenery of the Olympics at the main studio," according to the reporter. One of our demonstration members, gave a brief demonstration. With a short and strong kihap, he jumped on the spot, turned in the air, and with a kick, burst two balloons with both his feet. The balloons popped with a 'pang pang!' and he landed on his feet. The people who had gathered around us like bees cheered joyfully. The reporter broadcasted the uplifted festival atmosphere of the Olympic park for about 5 minutes. When the broadcast was over, even the police officers who had been following us around changed their attitudes, applauding and shaking hands with us. Thinking this was our chance, we asked the police if we could do some demonstrations, with the assurance that we wouldn't cause trouble. At first, they refused apologetically, but after discussing amongst themselves, the officers told us that they'd allow it for just a bit while they protected us. The police officers, armed with protective armor, pistols, surrounded us in a circle and made an impromptu stage for us to demonstrate. Visitors from all over the world cheered and loved it. For them, it was finally a proper festive atmosphere. After the demonstration, we took pictures together, and some tourists handed us small badges or props—souvenirs from their own country. It was a moment and place where everyone became one, beyond nationality, and all because of Taekwondo.

However, the very next week, there was a bombing in that exact place. This terrorist attack turned the world upside down, with two people dead and around 100 people injured. I saw the scene of the bombing on TV, and it was where I had stood the week before. I shuddered at the thought that everyone that day could have been in grave danger. I thought on how even the many, fully-armed police forces could not stop a bombing, and how perhaps civilian peacemakers like us may contribute more to human peace than military forces.

The English Tsunami Finally Stormed in

Any easy-going thoughts of being employed even without solid English skills crashed down in my final year of university. Back home in Korea, I applied to a major company. With 30 people going for 1 job, the 1st, 2nd and 3rd parts of the application all consisted of an English writing exam, an English listening exam, and an English-speaking interview. Of course, I was turned down. I reached the conclusion that I needed to learn English to survive, and quickly. 'But how? Let's drown in a sea of English!' I decided to move to America. And besides, wasn't my childhood dream to become an international Taekwondo instructor?

During the Atlanta Olympics, we dropped by the city of Chattanooga, Tennessee, two hours away from Atlanta to do a demonstration at a Korean Church. I remembered that the church had asked if we could send an instructor that could teach Korean and Taekwondo. I got ahold of their number with much difficulty and called the church. The church told me that they would give me a religious work visa. Elated, I quickly decided that I would go. I worked a part-time job until I could afford a plane ticket. I kept it a secret from everyone, until right before leaving for America. "Surprise!" As I thought, everyone was indeed surprised. "You're terrible at English, why of all places America?"

Chapter 2: Stumbling Test Flight

Finally, to America!

Immediately after my graduation, I got onto the plane with only a backpack. I wasn't going with the aim to study abroad or to succeed as a Taekwondo Instructor. It was just a road that I had impulsively decided on, thinking that I would stay there for about a year, explore a new world, and learn some English. I thought that I would automatically learn English with ease if I just lived there for a year or so. And with that skill, I would be able to open the door to employment. Looking back, it could have been the beginning of a tragedy, forged from ultimate ignorance.

My father repeatedly advised me: "You're a Taekwondo Instructor. Don't do anything to embarrass your country, don't try to make money, and exalt Korea in the sight of all!" I didn't realize it back then, but this would be the advice that I would hold closest to my heart all throughout my time in America.

Hearing that I was leaving for America, an acquaintance asked me if I could deliver something to his younger brother. At the Gimpo Airport International Office, I was getting anxious as the boarding time was approaching but the person had not yet arrived. Finally, he ran towards me. He handed me a black bag, in which he claimed there were shoes and other miscellaneous household goods. Hastily, I hurried to board the plane. I imagined all sorts of things as I crossed the Pacific. 'I shall come back having mastered English! I will make friends with American people!'

I arrived at San Francisco International Airport and went to customs after completing the entry procedure. Did my face give off a wrong impression? I was stopped at customs. I unpacked all my bags. The customs officer pulled out a tightly tied-up black plastic bag from the unpacked load and asked what it was. I felt faint. It wasn't mine. It would be problematic if I said I didn't know. Entering the country with someone else's property was illegal. But I didn't know what was inside....

The officer seemed suspicious seeing my hesitant expression and immediately started to unravel the plastic bag. I became even more anxious. I needed to answer before he opened the bag! But suddenly, I got a hunch. The shape of the plastic bag looked like a rolled-up rubber hose. 'But no way, there's no way, right? You wouldn't do that to something who's going to America?' When the customs officer untied the plastic bag to look in, he screamed and threw his head backward. "Ack! What is this?" I answered immediately. "Korean food, soondae!" (Soondae is a Korean sausage made from stuffing cow or pig intestines with blood and noodles, among other things.) The customs officer stood with both hands stretched out in fear. The smell that came out of the black bag... I was right! I was more-or-less kicked out of the airport with the bag of soondae. 'Ah, how humiliating. Out of everything he could send me off with, how could he ask me to deliver soondae? I could have been kicked out of the country, denied entry!' From the start, my rough entry process seemed to be an omen of my unknown future.

Korean Language School Taekwondo

I started teaching Taekwondo in America at a Korean language School. Even though I say "school," it was, in fact, a weekend day care for Korean-Americans from kindergarten age to high school students. Rather than age, the classes were divided by students' Korean language level. Little kids who have yet to go to school speak Korean rather well because they spend so much time at home with their grandmothers or mothers. But as they grow up and start attending school, they use more English than Korean and soon forget how to speak Korean. Dividing Korean language school classes by level meant that a kindergartener and a high school student could be put together in the same class. Therefore, no matter how much you teach them, the class progress goes around in circles.

In a Korean language school where most children can't speak Korean very well, communication among myself and the children in the mandatory Taekwondo class was challenging. I couldn't speak English, and the children couldn't speak Korean. At first, the children seemed so rude to me. They would talk back to my instructions, saying "I don't get it."

"Enough! What brats! What do you take Taekwondo for! All of you, get down!" The children didn't even know what that meant. I told showed them first and told them to copy me. All the children lay down on the floor, and I brought my bamboo sword down on them, regardless of gender. The spanked children's eyes grew wide with shock. To the kids who were starting to cry, I shouted. "You're crying? Fine, cry! The ones who cry will get another hit! How dare you look down on Taekwondo?" The children swallowed their cries in surprise at my bellow. Even the parents who were watching couldn't say anything because I was too confident. Once, a teenage girl who played the piano accompaniment at church did 100 push-ups because she couldn't follow instructions correctly. She couldn't play the piano for the next few days because her arms hurt, and the choir's head scolded me.

Anyway, the children hated Taekwondo class and did not follow me well. In the Taekwondo class that their parents pushed them into, the Instructor who didn't even speak English kept on enforcing punishment like some disciplinary committee head. Naturally, the children would not be led anywhere. With no progress made in class, I felt frustrated and even felt resentful of the seemingly useless children.

Then one day I realized, 'I shout at the children to learn Korean while living in America where they don't use Korean a lot, while I can't even speak a word of English properly.' I felt like I had come to my senses. What right did I have to treat the poor kids like this? Afterward, I tried my best to get close to the children. I completely quit whacking them and gave them as little discipline as possible. Apart from during Taekwondo class, I stood up for the children every time in the school or church. I gradually became friends with the children. Later, the kids, big or small, started clinging to me whenever they saw me. Once I got close to them, I couldn't help but realize how dear and adorable they were. But I still taught Taekwondo class with strict authority and cold airs, without even a trace of a smile on my face. The children would ask me, "Master, why are you so different during Taekwondo class?"

I never learned Taekwondo in a "fun" way. From a young age, I was elected to be a member of the elite team, trained with the very best, and grew up as the school- and then the state-representative. I had never smiled during Taekwondo time and had never once talked back to my Master. I grew up in a generation where Taekwondo training was incredibly strict. Even the harshest training had to be done if ordered. Nosebleeds and broken arms were just everyday occurrences. So, it was no wonder I didn't know how to teach Taekwondo in an enjoyable way. I was lacking confidence in myself, too. "Because Taekwondo is Taekwondo! Now, all of you gather up! Line up side to side!"

The children always crowded around me, asking "Master Lee, buy us ice cream!" Even after tightening my belt as much as possible, there was very little money I could spare. But I would still put some money aside to buy the children ice cream. And when the children smiled happily at the treats, nothing seemed to be more important. In those moments I was their favorite "Master." The time I spent with the children who would come running and cling to me was like fresh spring water amidst an exhausting life.

Although it was a Korean language school, the school also taught skills such as classical dance, traditional musical instruments, and opened free

Taekwondo classes for residents to provide a service to the local community while promoting Korean culture. Amongst neighboring Americans, some people became more interested in Korea after learning Taekwondo and decided to register themselves at the Korean language school to learn the Korean language. To the adults in this group, I gave up my spare time for private Taekwondo lessons. I also spent time organizing church youth demonstration groups. They were young people who had never learned Taekwondo before, but as result of training each person with a special skill, they were able to cover each other's weaknesses and highlight their strengths. The children's demonstration team and youth demonstration team regularly performed Taekwondo in various places such as nursing homes, homeless shelters, and street festivals.

For their school presentations, the students would show off Taekwondo moves. Unlike other students presenting on general subjects such as musical instruments, sports, etc., our students would wear their uniforms and demonstrate on the spot, while they explained Taekwondo and promoted Korea. Of course, it was very popular, and the students would receive good grades.

When asked by local schools or social organizations if we could introduce them to Korean culture, I brought the children to demonstrate. I would have them put on their uniforms under their hanbok, traditional Korean formal attire, and the students would start off with a traditional dance. Then they would immediately take off the hanbok and show Taekwondo demonstrations while yelling kihap. Unsurprisingly, this demonstration twist was very well received. Seeing the enthusiasm from watching the Taekwondo demonstrations, I felt that there was nothing that could appeal to people about Korean culture as strongly Taekwondo. It was rewarding for me to work as a civilian cultural envoy. Nevertheless, my schedule was overloaded with no time to rest, from working at the Korean language school, teaching Taekwondo, and leading demonstrations.

A Challenge from a Neighboring Dojang Demonstration Team

Our church pastor once asked a middle-aged Korean woman to come to visit our church, to evangelize her. She replied that she recently received her 1st-degree black belt, and was too busy teaching Taekwondo at a neighboring dojang. Our pastor told her that our church also had a Master from Korea, and suggested she could come by and help educate our students as well. And the woman said, "How much could a church Taekwondo school do?" and asked the pastor for a chance to organize a demonstration at our church, saying that her dojang's demonstration team would drop by sometime. The dojang that the woman attended was the top dojang in our city.

One Sunday, after church service and lunch, I was teaching Taekwondo. Suddenly a crowd of Americans wearing white uniforms and black belts poured into the church gym. Around 30 black belts and their families came in all together, and soon the church gym was filled with 80 to 90 Americans. When I asked how I could help them, they answered that they were to have a demonstration at my church gym that day. I had not received any notice beforehand. The head of the team was a Master named Roy, who had a handsome mustache like the action actor Chuck Norris. He introduced himself as a 4th degree black belt. I greeted him as politely as possible, but he returned it with stiff acknowledgment. I was 5th degree back then. It bothered me that someone—with less training experience than I had, no less—barged into another Master's class without any notification and did not even bother to say hello properly. Nevertheless, I wrapped up the class and sat the children down, telling them that black belts from a neighboring dojang had visited to demonstrate so they should watch and learn. At the time, the highest belt amongst the children was a blue belt.

They put on some loud music and started the demonstration. They only demonstrated forms poom-sae, one step sparring. For breaking, they just broke one board with a basic kick and hand technique. The highest-level kick shown was breaking three boards with a jumping back kick. They applauded and screamed amongst themselves as if at a festival. At the time, I had experience in my career as part of the National Representative Demonstration Team of Korea, elected and sent by the World Taekwondo Headquarters, Kukkiwon. And back in those days, there was a world of difference in level between a United States Demonstration team and a Korean Demonstration team.

Finally, Master Roy appeared. Everyone tensed, and so did I. He had one board that he glared at for a long time in this particular stance. I couldn't for the life of me guess from his stance, with what he would break the board. 'What can he do in that stance? Is there a special technique that I have yet to know of?' "Ah-ha!" With an impressive shout, a reverse-knife hand strike… The whole demonstration team and their families applauded and went frenzy. It was absurd.

Anyway, since they had finished the demonstration, I asked him to give some kind words to our children. "Taekwondo is a great martial art. If you learn it well, your life can change. So, if possible, don't learn it somewhere like this, but come to our dojang and learn it properly!" That was the gist of his speech. They were about to leave right after the speech, so I called out. "You came all the way here. We don't have much prepared, but we'd like to return the favor by showing something, too. Could you give us some of your time?" The people who were about to leave sat down again.

At that time, there were no special boards for breaking. You would buy a 1-inch thick wooden plank from building material stores and cut it into boards with a chainsaw. I took out the boards and randomly called out students, yellow belt or blue belt, boys or girls, to break them on the spot. Jumping over obstacles and side-kick, jumping spin hook-kick, tornado kick, stepping on the wall then jump kick, jumping three-way kick. "Crack! Crack! Crack!" The audience began to realize something was wrong. Later, I heard that a school friend of my blue belt student was in that demonstration team and that she was crestfallen. Her blue belt friend was doing board-breaking techniques that even she couldn't do.

Moreover, our church also had a female Master who used to be a Korean National player. She was a talented person who also coached the Singapore women's national Taekwondo team. She used to be a Master in another city, and had just moved here after marriage and had started attending our church. The audience turned upside down as the small woman stepped up and broke several surrounding boards "Pa-pa-pa! Pow, Pow!" in the blink of an eye.

Next it was my turn. I broke a 5-inch-thick board with a punch. Then breaking boards with a fingertip thrust, knife hand, reverse knife hand. "Crack! Crack! Crack!" I brought out a knife from the kitchen and stuck an apple on it in front of everyone, and crushed it by doing a tornado kick with bare feet. The black belt team's mouths all hung open.

I bowed politely once again. "There wasn't much to show you because we weren't prepared, but if an opportunity arises, we would also like to visit your dojang and do some demonstrations."

Apparently, Master Roy had heard that the church was teaching Taekwondo and thought if they did a good demonstration, he could get a lot of new students. His arrogant assumption and lack of information had only led to humiliation. The woman who had a big part in bringing the team to the church gym seemed to be uneasy and somewhat mortified. They were under the name of a Taekwondo dojang, but I couldn't help wondering what their students think Taekwondo is.

Since I hadn't lost anything, I soon forgot about the incident until much later. I decided to pay a visit to the dojang and say hello. If needed, I thought I could help Master Roy, too. An elegant, elderly lady was wearing a black belt and working as a manager. She was 2nd degree black belt. As soon as I walked in, she welcomed me respectfully, while she held my hand and said she enjoyed my demonstration last time. She told me about how since that day the black belts kept trying to step onto the wall and jump kick to the point that she was afraid the wall might eventually get holes! Master Roy had wrapped bandages around his finger and glared at the board to do the fingertip thrust, but in the end, gave up. She then proceeded to introduce me with high compliments to the surrounding parents.

Master Roy was in the middle of overseeing class. He glanced at me and quickly looked away. I was going to wait to say hello, but as soon as the class ended, he immediately started his next class. 'Ah! I guess it could look like I'm trying to pick a fight with him.' So I respectfully bowed from the back and left. The incident must have hurt master Roy's pride because even afterward when we would pass by each other, he would avoid me. It reaffirmed to me once again that I must always be humble. In this world, are there not so many martial artists that are at a higher place than me? One should not needlessly act pridefully, only to be embarrassed.

Breaking Bricks on the "Wrong Side of Town"

Much later, I worked at a gas station store in a rough part of town. One of my student's parents died from gun violence. It wasn't much of an exaggeration to say that we were living in a neighborhood as harsh as a battlefield. The store I worked at got robbed often. There were gunshot holes all over, on the store walls and the ceilings. From time to time there would even be shootings right in front of the store. Someone would shoot like mad at a passing car, but the police would never show up. If you asked the shooter, he'd say that the car driver had run away without paying for the drugs. So, there were drug dealers, too. In that neighborhood, the young people dreamed of becoming drug dealers, of carrying around a bundle of cash in their pockets. People would swear and grab each other by the collar and fight like dogs over the smallest of matters. Addicted to alcohol and drugs, it was hard to find someone sane there. Drunkards dressed in shabby clothes would stagger past the poorly lit street lamps in front of our store and scream incomprehensible nothings, day and night.

I was immediately harassed when I first started working at the store. No one thought twice about hazing me, the "new Asian dude" who was naïve as to how things worked in the neighborhood. Usually, it was by throwing down money that wasn't enough. If I complained, the immediate response would be a middle finger. And then they would pour out a stream of high-pitched and clipped swearwords. At first, it was okay. But as time passed, I steadily started to understand what they were saying, and it grew harder to tolerate.

These people would snatch things from the store without paying, yelling at me to put it on a tab. If they were caught stealing items under their clothes, they would just loudly argue without remorse, because wasn't it fine since they hadn't left the store yet? Sometimes after getting caught, they would throw the items on the floor or stomp on them and destroy them. There were also plenty of people who would grab whole boxes of beers or snacks and make a run for it. If I tried to stop them, they'd pull out a knife or pat the gun in their pocket, and threaten that no one would know if they killed an Asian like me. Occasionally even if I caught someone outright stealing, bystanders would defend him instead. I'd be lucky even to get the stolen item back. It was that rough of a neighborhood.

There were a group of men that hung out all day in front of the store, trying to pick fights. Amongst them, the leader was a man called Morris. He was a big and muscular man, around 6 feet, 3 inches tall. He was uneducated but had quite a silver tongue. He would swear and attack me several times a day and casually eat food straight from the store shelves. Property damage was an everyday occurrence, and he would spread open all the newspapers for sale and throw them on the floor. If I said something about it, he would reply, "What's an Asian like you going to do? You'll be found dead tonight!" He would then make a finger pistol and pretend to shoot at me, making gunshot noises with his mouth.

"Bang!" Those who have experienced it will know that this feels seriously threatening. But I couldn't swear back or call the police. If I resisted too much, he would stand in front of the store and scare customers away. So, I had to consider it as paying street tax to endure most of his behavior. After some time, the fact that I was a Taekwondo Master became known around the neighborhood. But I only got sneered at even further. "Whatcha going to do with karate? I could kick your ass with one punch." Any East Asian martial arts used to be karate in people's eyes. I endured and endured to the point where I was just about to explode. I became determined that I had to settle this, dead or alive.

Morris limped on his left leg. It was his weakness, so I planned to use it to my advantage by aiming a kick at his left leg. A giant of a man he may have been, but I wasn't exactly weak either. I had broken ax handles with my roundhouse kick. But just as I was about to confront him, I caught him rolling his trousers up while drinking. Instead of a leg, a steel pipe was attached to his shoes, working as an artificial leg. 'Uh, bad plan!' No matter how angry I was, to kick at an artificial leg was too cowardly. Later I heard that Morris also used to be a well-known drug dealer in the neighborhood, until his whole leg under the knee was blown off by a competitor's shotgun. Disabled, bitter anger was the only thing left in the man.

That day too, Morris and his followers had been playing all kinds of tricks against me throughout the day. I finally lost it and shouted. "Hey! Follow me out, all of you!" "What's crawled up his butt?" All of them followed me out in. Red bricks, coated with bits of cement and frozen from the rain, were scattered all over the place on the side of the crumbling wall. I picked up one of them and looked around. A piling stood next to the gas pump. I put the brick on top of it, yelled out a long kihap and gathered all my strength, and brought my knife hand down. "Aaah-hah!" With a "wham!" the brick broke. It wasn't just broken cleanly into two pieces either. The broken half that fell to the frozen concrete ground smashed into pieces. I turned back towards the group and roared, "Bring it on, you bastards!" Morris and his lackeys all took a step backward. Their jaws had dropped, and their eyes were wide open in shock.

There was a short silence, and then Morris shouted, "Master Lee!" That was the first time Morris had called me anything respectful. Until then my name to him had been "this bastard" and "that bastard," followed by a stream of swear words. "Master Lee, are your hands okay?" "Are you kidding? Of course, it's okay!" Morris asked me if he could touch my hands. Then he proceeded to hold my hands, seemingly at loss of what to do. My hands were red and burning, but I was flustered more than anything. "What's with the change of attitude?" Morris and his group picked up broken brick pieces from the ground and excitedly held them out to passersby. At that moment, suddenly, I was their friend.

After that day, whenever I arrived at the store to work, Morris would be waiting. He would stand and greet me in a friendly manner. "Nothing much happened today. A few guys made a bit of a fuss, so I just talked to them and sent them away." "Thank you, Morris." "Nah, it's what friends do!" And I would start my work shift. Then, that horrible and frightening neighborhood became a somewhat familiar and likable place.

Still, someone would inevitably pick a fight. He would throw down a few pennies at the counter, and demand something. "That's not enough money. You have to pay the right price, or I can't give it to you." I'd reply, smiling. "I said I don't have it. Do you want to die? How dare you!" The atmosphere would turn harsh, and he'd be about to grab my collar. Then Morris would come in from his usual spot outside the store, and strike the back of the offender's head. "Wham!" "Are you dying to get killed? Do you know who this is? He can break bricks with his bare hands. Is your head harder than a brick?" "Him? Ha-ha, no way." And then another hit from Morris. "Wham!" "Bastard! I'm saying I saw it!" 'He deserved that. I feel vindicated now!' But instead of saying that aloud I would smoothly say, "Morris, stop it, it's all right. You're being too harsh." "It's because he's doesn't believe me. The bastard's asking for it!" Then the offender would have no choice to pay the remaining money and leave.

Afterward, I came to understand Morris better as a human. He can't help but live that way. Who wouldn't want to have a happy and comfortable life? But being abandoned in an environment like that doesn't leave one with many choices.

Chef Scott and His Sandwich

In the corner of the store, we had a kitchen that sold fried chicken. I got into a fight with its chef, Scott. I say chef, but the chicken wasn't really what you would call cooking. He would just split raw chicken, cover it with frying powder, and fry it in oil, simple as that. Every time, he would secretly sell fried chickens behind our backs for 1 or 2 dollars and keep the money for himself. Sometimes he would hide a whole box of the raw chicken ingredients in the trash bins and then sell them somewhere else for a few dollars. Whatever I said to try to stop him was ignored. Soon after I became angry and told him that he should quit working in the kitchen if he continued like this, but he was shamelessly audacious about his wrong-doings.

"You're not even the owner, what's it to you? Do you want to die? I heard you do some karate, is that why you're messing around? Come here, and I'll cut you into pieces!" Scott pointed at me with his chicken-cutting knife. "You bastard, I said it's Taekwondo, not karate!" Admittedly, I overreacted in an unnecessary argument. It just shows that if you lack mind training, you do things that might get you killed. "You think I'm scared because you have a knife? OK! Bring it on, come at me!" I blocked the entrance to the kitchen. "You seriously have a dying wish, huh? Do you think I can't kill you without a knife?" "Don't make me laugh. I'm a Taekwondo Master. You can't compare to me with your bare hands! So, come at me with that knife, and that'll make it a fair fight that I can beat you up in!"

A customer in the store hollered to everyone outside about a fight. People who heard pushed their way inside. Finally, they murmured, they'd see the Asian guy's rumored skills! Everyone seemed excited. Well, you know what they say, there's nothing more entertaining than watching people fight. Scott's neck stuck to his shoulders, and his waist was thick. He was a muscular man with a lot of strength. One wild, careless punch in the wrong place, and I could be led straight to my afterlife. "Are you crazy? You're gonna die in pieces!" Malice passed over Scott's eyes, and the veins on his neck popped out. His knife cut the air, threatening me.

I guess if you have nothing to lose, the only thing you are left with is reckless bravery. I was like that. 'Ugh, whatever! I don't know anymore!" I yelled even louder, "Hurry up and come on out! We're going to settle this today, dead or alive!" But as angry I may have been, I couldn't start a fight with this man, furious as a bull and with a knife in his hand, in the kitchen. Not when the kitchen floor was drenched with all the oil and grease 365 days a year, to the point where I would slip even if I were walking across. I had to lure him outside first. And then I figured I'd avoid the knife, attack with something short and intense, like a front kick or back kick, and aim for a vital spot. And risk my life in the process. But I would aim for his windpipe with a spear fingertip thrust. If I thrust as I would at a breaking board, it could cut through his throat. Either way, for both knife-holding Scott and myself, a single attack would determine the outcome of this fight.

"What are you waiting for? Come on out! I'll beat you up and say it was self-defense!" In response to my flying off the handle, Scott warned, "You're not leaving this town alive today!" "Don't worry, you bastard! I don't have anyone to care if I die, so bring it on!" At this point, he seemed suddenly nervous, because he looked around the audience and started subtly asking for help. "Hey, you guys are just gonna watch a friend fight?" But unlike usual, no one interfered. On the contrary, they seemed to be expecting something impressive to happen. "Go on, fight, you even got a knife!" As the mood turned strange, Scott began to back out. "They say martial artists are good at self-control, why do you get carried away so quickly?" "You started it! Why, scared? OK! I won't kill you, I'll just crush an arm or a leg, so hurry up and get out!" At that, I could see the fear in Scott's eyes.

Scott wasn't the only problem though. Everyone was only edging us on to fight, and the surrounding onlookers were blocking any space to retreat. The small store could end up in a bloodbath. Just in time, the store owner who had stepped out ran back into the store after seeing all the commotion. "Master Lee! What's happening? If you explode here, we're all in big trouble! Please just bear with it, please!" The owner pushed me out. The audience who had lost a good show protested, "Just let them fight!"

The incident that day just wrapped itself up like that. But after calming down, I started worrying about what would happen the next day. What if he picks another fight? I walked into the store, tense, but Scott flinched in surprise when he saw me. I didn't look either and pretended to ignore him. Soon he came up to me and handed me a chicken sandwich, with a generous portion of chicken and even a leaf of lettuce. He was the first to apologize for the day before. Relieved, I also quickly apologized back. "I lost my temper yesterday, and it wasn't how a martial artist should have behaved. I'm sorry. We're colleagues, let's not fight like that again." I shook his hands, grinning, and took a big bite out of his chicken sandwich. I had thought that it wouldn't be that good since he wasn't a real cook, but on the contrary, it was incredibly delicious. After the incident, it got much more comfortable to work – I somewhat gained a reputation, and a rumor circulated that "nothing good comes out of picking a fight with that guy."

That was already a long time ago, but there are times that I miss Scott's sandwich, with chicken breasts slathered inside. Sadly, I can't eat his sandwiches ever again. Sometime after the incident, Scott was working at a construction site to dismantle a building, and a wall crumbled onto him. I heard he was crushed to death. I felt empty and heart-broken. He was too young, and his death was too sudden. They say that people come into our lives because we are destined to meet. Whether friend or enemy, we learn and grow up through these bonds. I could almost hear Scott telling me, "Life isn't a big deal! Don't be upset and live your life to the fullest!"

A Bet on a Cigarette

After learning faces of the customers, the neighborhood wasn't as scary. The people were rough, but once they accepted you as a friend, it became possible to keep up a sort of decent relationship. I was the annoying Asian who only came to the neighborhood to earn money, but if the store closed these people wouldn't have anywhere to immediately buy alcohol, cigarettes, milk, eggs and other random groceries. Most people didn't own a car so leaving town to do grocery shopping was also tricky.

One day, a guy I had never seen around before came into the store. He had tattoos nicely done on his rugged muscles, long braided hair and a short beard. 'Did he get out of jail?' If someone disappears around this neighborhood, they were most likely in jail. The guy suddenly pulled out a knife from his back pocket and stabbed down into the counter. "I need a cigarette!" He spoke with a low and rough voice and glaring eyes. But I knew how things worked here now. If they get away with it once, they'll be getting away with it forever. A few guys in the store giggled from behind. I took out a cigarette box and put it down firmly. I leaned over his knife to face him and said, "Yeah? Well, I need money!" A little nonplussed at my reaction, he glared at me but eventually asked, "How much is it?" before putting the money down. The guys from behind came up and smacked the man on the back of his head, laughing. I laughed together with them. Only the man was left feeling foolish.

Short, Simple, but Sure English

When I say I do Taekwondo, people would always ask, "Can you kill someone with your bare hands?" If I tell them no, they look down on my skills. If I say yes, then they treat me like some delinquent who learned Taekwondo for those kinds of reasons. It is a question filled with thorns. So, whenever someone asks, I answer shortly but firmly. "I don't want to!" People twitch at this and do not ask any more questions. I am saying I have the skills, but I choose not to. Sometimes, short English is the best medicine.

Fist Training at the Clothing Store

I once used to work at a shabby local clothing store. There were several tall and muscular clerks that worked with me. However, they'd always look the other way whenever someone shoplifted. Sometimes I noticed and reproached them for it, but they said that they couldn't help it. They worried that the shoplifters would take revenge on the way back home, for tattling on a neighbor. "So, you should catch the shoplifters," they'd say. That being said, it was not like these men were weak in any way. When they played basketball, I saw them easily doing dunk shots with their big physique. Their strength, speed, jump, and footwork were brilliant. Once I taught them how to do a front snap kick for fun, and the kick cut the air with deadly power. In their free time, they would often lift a 50-pound dumbbell a few dozen times.

When working in a stuffy clothing store, you usually get too exhausted to do any exercise. The only training, I could spare time for was fist training. When I had free time, I would walk around the store while hitting my fist with a wooden bat. My co-workers would watch with curiosity, and eventually, they wanted to try it out too. But with an untrained fist, the only result you'd get is aching bones and scraped skin. After attempting a few times, they wailed about the pain and gave up. I also showed them a photo of me breaking a brick with my first. Looking at the broken brick pieces, they seemed to imagine their heads in the place of the brick.

One lazy afternoon, we hadn't had any customers for hours. And then someone with "thief" practically written on his face walked in. I was chasing away sleep, noisily beating the wooden bat against my fist. Usually, when a customer comes in, I stop immediately in case some people feel threatened, but that day I spaced out a little. The customer walked towards one of my co-workers called Sean and exchanges a few words with him. Then for some reason he glanced at me, sighed deeply, and left the store shaking his head. "What's up? No size?" Sean replied lazily, "Nah, he wanted to shoplift and asked me to pretend not to see. So, I told him, 'I'm fine with it, but see that guy with the bat over there? He's been hitting his fist like that for the last 2 hours. Go ask him.' I said that, and he just left."

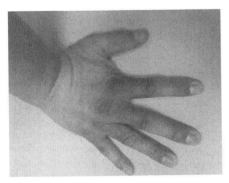 

Alaska, the Land of the Midnight Sun

I knew a 3rd-degree black belt junior who taught Taekwondo in Anchorage, Alaska. He'd been teaching quite a few years. He reached out to me and asked me if I could oversee a black belt promotion test. I am an officially licensed instructor by the World Taekwondo Headquarters, Kukkiwon, and have the authority to judge at a black belt promotion test. Since he said he would also pay for my flight, I agreed to go readily. It's part of the United States, but you have to cross Canada to reach Alaska. I departed from Atlanta by a direct, 9-hour flight and arrived at 11:30 pm. When I got off the plane, the sun was high up, as if it were only in the middle of the day. It was the infamous midnight sun. I went outside at 3 am and walked through the empty streets. The world was bright, yet I felt lonely and foreign as if all the people in the world had suddenly evaporated into nothingness. Usually, I can sleep anytime as soon as I close my eyes. Maybe it was because of the light coming in through the curtains, but somehow, I could not fall asleep quickly. After a fortnight like that, my face turned sallow, and even my organs seemed to malfunction. As a guest, I was treated to excellent food, but it was painful to eat it because I couldn't even digest properly. I wasn't even able to use the bathroom. I became exhausted even before the actual promotion test. I just wanted to get it done and leave quickly.

The day before the test, I had the students practice board breaking. They weren't even able to break a 1-inch board! I was confused. 'But even our kids can do this…' In the end, I asked my junior to show us a demonstration firsthand. After all, the instructor must set an example for the students to follow. I put three boards together and told him to do an elbow strike. He showed a good strike, but the boards wouldn't break. "Oh dear, you have to strike harder!" My junior gritted his teeth and struck again. With an ear-splitting sound, the boards broke. But my junior's face became distorted. His elbow was scraped and blood was flowing. 'Ouch, that must hurt!' Perhaps because the trees grew up in the harsh cold, the wood was unbelievably hard. It was then I realized that the strength of a wooden board could differ depending on the region. The test itself took place in a local YMCA dance room that had a wood floor. Starting with the basic movement and poom-sae, the students went through kicking, one-step sparring, self-defense, sparring. Finally, the last step was board breaking. Not unlike the day before, everyone was struggling to break the board.

As a guest instructor invited from afar, I had to encourage the participants and establish some standards for the testing. I had to break the boards. A simple yet appealing technique would be a fingertip thrust. 'It's just a 1-inch thick board.' I didn't think much of it and struck with my fingertips as usual. 'Wham!' The board broke, and a tsunami of pain started from my fingertips. I felt my nose water, my eyes blinded with tears. It hurt like nothing else. I quickly held my hands together behind my back. "So breaking board is all about confidence, and…." I didn't even know what I was saying. My hands hurt terribly, and all my focus went to my hands behind my back. Blood was pooling and dripping down from my closed fist. 'Argh, Alaska's boards are really solid!' But it seemed like it wasn't for nothing because board breaking went well for everyone after that.

Alaska has spectacular scenery of glaciers breaking down, is rich in seafood, and has a beautiful aurora during winter. Koreans go to the northernmost village in Alaska to run their business. I couldn't help respecting them for their strength, for going to the very edge of the globe to make their lives. It's probably through this kind of gumption that the power of Korea spreads worldwide. Anyway, thanks to Taekwondo, I was able to look around the end of the earth, and for that I am grateful.

English Doesn't Automatically Learn Itself

Even living in America, if you don't study, you can't learn English. I learned to speak and understand English with time, but my reading and writing skills were always static. There's a limit to comprehending and learning vocabulary if you don't read a lot of books. You might even struggle with just writing an email. And naturally, conversation with Americans becomes limited. I found that reading was the best shortcut for me to learn English. It didn't even matter if they were easy books. For example, I got familiar with the language by reading Garfield, a comic strip about a troublemaker cat. Perhaps because of this, even now when I explain something in English, my students tell me, "Master Lee, you talk like a cartoon character!"

Self-Defense Taught by a Cleaner

At night, I also worked as a cleaner in empty buildings. Cleaners are not the only people who work at night, though. Security guards also work at night. It might seem easy, but it's a job that switches your day and night and can put the guard in a risky situation. It's not a very good job, as it often comes with poor treatment and low salaries. But a guard will learn faces, make small talk, and become friendly with the nighttime cleaners. One building I cleaned was very strict security-wise. However, despite that, the security guards for this building walked around with only a flashlight and did not know any necessary self-defense techniques. When they found out I was a Taekwondo instructor, they asked me to teach them a skill. I had been grateful towards them for treating me kindly, so I agreed to teach them a few techniques every night after cleaning. They would practice together all night. When I checked on them the next night, I could see that they'd practiced earnestly. After a few months, they rose to a decent level. The security guards thanked me sincerely. They lamented that they wanted to learn more when they had more time.

Word got around and the mall security guard of a neighboring building joined in. He would wait until I left my building to throw away the trash and learn techniques from me one by one in a dark alley. Later on, I did feel slightly tired, as I was busy enough cleaning and thought I was losing time over these free lessons. But, in fact, I unknowingly had the favor returned by these people. These security guards don't just protect the buildings: they also manage the buildings at night. Among other things, they make reports on the cleaning and the cleaner's work attitude. If they report negatively, it's difficult to get hired again as a cleaner. But these security guards gave me very positive reviews while I was working. Thanks to them, I could sign an extended contract without trouble.

One mall security guard later even visited our Korean language school and joined us in Taekwondo class. He was an excellent learner. Through his connections, we were invited to give a Taekwondo demonstration during a Christmas event at the local mall. Our Korean language school students demonstrated under the spotlights in the middle of the mall. Even the security guard joined in, wearing his security guard uniform, and showed off the self-defense skills he had learned in the dark. Other security guards and shop owners were amazed, wondering when he'd learned everything. After the demonstration, he picked up and carried a stone I had broken with my hands, boasting that his Master had come from far east. He gradually learned to be more self-confident and applied for the job that he always wanted as a correctional officer. He later thanked me, saying that he got accepted because of his experience in martial arts. It was a position of a higher salary, but also higher risk due to the prisoners. Therefore, self-defense skills were necessary. He had leaped from being a nighttime security guard to a proud government employee, thanks to Taekwondo.

Severed Ligament for the Second Time

In a park where the Tennessee River flows, the International Culture Festival took place. Teams from Europe and Asia showed their folk dances and performed traditional music endlessly. It was a colorful event, where the American culture team showed Cherokee Indian dance and played jazz music. Our Korean language school was also invited to participate in the Korean culture performances. The children dressed up in colorful traditional clothing and presented a puppet dance and a fan dance. Immediately after the fan dance, they threw off their hanboks to reveal their Taekwondo uniforms. We gave a team demonstration, showing one-step sparring and board breaking. The audience loved it. After a long string of dances and music performances, having wooden boards break and children yelling out kihap was a lively change of pace. Soon it was my turn. I finished a few self-defense and breaking moves. Next, I stuck an apple on a knife and did a tornado kick. I missed. It was stiflingly hot weather, and not only was I physically tired from waiting my turn, but the ground was also uneven. The audience was enjoying themselves, laid back on the grass, but for me who was representing Korean culture to everyone, it felt like a colossal mistake.

Once again, I jumped forward but my foot slipped on the grass, and my body fell backward. I knew the angle of my body was wrong, but it was already late to retract my foot. I kicked the knife blade directly from below. The apple smashed into pieces and flew away, but I felt a chilling sensation on the top of my foot. I quickly turned around and picked up my shoes. If I showed my injury, I would dampen the mood of the festival. Blood began to fill and squelch in my shoes, and the pain on my foot was reaching my bones. I was horrified but didn't show it outwardly. I wrapped up the demonstration quickly and drove back to the Korean language school with my injured foot. I had done the same demonstration during my senior year in university. I kicked the knife with the apple and ended up with a severed ligament. It was at a freshman orientation event that took place for two days and three nights at a mountain resort. As a student leader of the Natural Science department, I wanted to show something cool and did an impulsive demonstration on the spot. I made a reckless decision and called out a random female student to hold up the knife. The nervous student squeezed her eyes shut and turned the knife blade towards the direction of my foot, and a ligament got severed. The knife flew towards the audience, but fortunately, there was no one injured but myself. It was in the middle of the night, and I was in a position of responsibility regarding the event, so I kept quiet and bled all night. The next day, I went to the hospital, had surgery, and was hospitalized for a month. It was that exact spot that I injured at the International Culture Festival.

When I came back to the school, I looked at my foot. My white sock had been dyed red all the way up to the ankle. The blood kept flowing out of the deep knife cut. I couldn't stop the bleeding nor could I move my big toe. "My ligament is severed again!" The father of a student saw me, and horrified, he drove me at once to the emergency room.

The call doctor for that weekend inspected my foot, poking and prodding at my injury with a pincer. Digging at a knife wound with a metal pincer just felt like torture. But to save face as a Master, I bit my tongue and endured the pain. Someone who had been watching from the side asked, "Master Lee, doesn't it hurt?" "Yes, but it's bearable." His next words almost gave me a heart attack. "Wow, you're incredible. And I can see bones, too!" "Ugh!"

The doctor concluded that a ligament on the top of my foot was indeed severed, and this would require a specialist to come in. In the meantime, I had to go through all these basic examinations that honestly didn't seem necessary to me. As if all the blood I spilled today wasn't enough, the hospital drew blood from me again. And then a blood pressure test, and so many questions! It felt like such a terrible waste of money to me. A specialist came in and inspected the injury again. "You cut your bones too. What did you do?" "I kicked a knife with my barefoot." "What? Why would you do that?" "I'm a Taekwondo instructor. I had a demonstration today." He was happy to know that, telling me that he also used to learn Taekwondo. "But what's this? I haven't done anything yet, but there's already a surgical scar here." I felt pathetic as I replied, "This is my second time." Dumbfounded, he said, "Shouldn't you switch your lifestyle around a little?" "I think so, too. I'll switch and kick with my other foot next time," I joked, but then anxiously asked if I would fully recover. Since it was not even my first surgery but my second, at the very best I would recover 70% of my foot's functionality. I would not be able to run as well as before, and I might even limp a little when walking... I received surgery under general anesthesia. When I opened my eyes, my leg was thoroughly bandaged, with only two crutches left by my side.

My Dear Hometown Mother

In times of hardship, I sometimes have painful dreams. I see my hometown and I see my dear mother whom I haven't seen in years. In the midst of a heartwarming conversation, my mother gets up and leaves to go somewhere. No matter how much I call her and try to catch up, she goes farther and farther away. When I wake up with a start, I am lying down, alone in the utter darkness. My heart sinks. 'Where am I? What am I doing here alone?' All of a sudden, a wave of loneliness and sadness swallows me up with the darkness. I missed my mother so very much. What if my mother was telling me she was well only to reassure me through the phone, just as I do for her? At least when I joined the army, I could look up at the stars and take comfort from the fact she was somewhere under the southern sky. Now she was on the other side of the world, where we couldn't even look up at the same sky. I couldn't run to her if I wanted to. My hometown was in a land that I could now only reach by crossing the United States continent westward and then the Pacific Ocean. On days that I dreamt of my mother, I would spend the whole night awake, aching to see her again.

Chapter 3: New Challenge

A Worm Meets His Other

There was a Korean college student who learned Taekwondo from me. One day, she told me, "Master Lee, I met a Korean senior student today in the library, and I thought you two would look great together. You have to meet her!" She put in a lot of effort, going back and forth between the young lady and myself. I agreed to meet her because of my student's enthusiasm. I arrived at the meeting place. It was pleasant, having a charming female student smiling and listen to my banal stories. I walked her back home. She lived in the home of a 94-year-old American grandmother, taking care of her in exchange for a room. Several American college students each had a room in a gorgeous and old-fashioned house, taking turns to care for the bed-ridden old lady. At first it seemed like they were only staying there because of the free rooms. However, as soon as we entered the house, this Korean girl ran to the old lady lying in her bed; she smiled warmly as she served her food and massaged her sore places. And she would chat about her day and everything that happened with the old lady at her bedside. She was as good as a real granddaughter. The old lady loved her presence. That scene captured my heart. But the young lady had said she would be transferring to a university in Florida a week later.

Since there was not much time left, I visited her for at least an hour each night from the very next day on. Even though it was a date, we just walked around her house and shared stories. But then she suddenly said to me, "Are you hurt? Why are you limping?" "Who? Me?" That was when I noticed my shadow, long from the moonlight, was swaying with each step I took. My heart sank. A year had passed since I had the ligament surgery, but I had never looked closely at my gait. I gave her the excuse of being slightly injuring from Taekwondo training, said my goodbyes, and went back home. I couldn't sleep. The next day, during Taekwondo class, I called over a random student. I said, "I'm going to walk straight across this line, so watch closely." Then I walked back and forth on the line. I asked, "Am I limping?" At first, she tilted her head in confusion, but her expression suddenly became stiff. And she ran away crying, "I don't know!"

'Oh...I really am limping.' I felt suffocated. They say that youth is happy, but that happiness didn't seem to belong to me.

The day before she left, I told the young lady that I couldn't ask her not to go, but I would always wait here. That she could come back whenever she needed a break from studying. That I would be a nest, a home where she could come back to rest her tired wings. That if she ever came to me, I would stand by her and support her in the pursuit of her studies. After a brief silence, she replied that if she ever came back, she would consider it as God's will and marry me. The next morning, she left without leaving even an address. But after many ups and downs, the young lady came back to my side. We had a small and simple wedding ceremony with the help of people around us, in this foreign land without our parents. Her American academic advisor walked her down the aisle instead of her father, and the 94-year-old grandmother sat in a wheelchair in place of her mother. And the young lady who married me that day is still my wife.

After that, my wife worked hard for ten years, continuously studying while helping me with my schooling. She completed the long process of her education with a full scholarship. I'm so proud of my wife, who endured such a difficult path without complaint. Thirteen years into our marriage, I think I have kept my promise to her before marriage. When she was a graduate student, we were a long-distance couple. When she was studying for her doctorate, I would wait for her to come back for one month during summer and one month during winter. Even now, we live apart during school semesters as my wife teaches at a State University in California, and we live together only during breaks. Even so, my wife and I believe that we are a match made in heaven. I asked her later, "What made you accept my proposal?" My wife replied, "That limping shadow under the moonlight felt so sad; I decided I would have to live out my life with you out of compassion."

Sabrina and Fingertip Breaking

There was a student Taekwondo club at the university my wife attended. When my wife introduced me to her friends as a Taekwondo Master, they asked if I could supervise their team. So, I visited once a week to teach them, like a volunteer. Their team captain was a senior student named Sabrina, a 1st degree ATA (American Taekwondo Association) black belt. Sabrina was the only black belt, and the rest ranged from white belts to red belts. Before I came along, Sabrina would rent the school gym and teach them basic level Taekwondo techniques. So naturally, when I visited, the students were very excited and could follow me well. Once we became closer, the members frequently came over to our house to hang out with us. A few months later, they said they were going to demonstrate at an elementary school affiliated with the university and asked me for help. I organized a demonstration plan that fit the team's level and trained them. When they asked me where they could get the wooden boards, I answered that I go to a construction material store to buy a 1-inch thick wood and have it cut accordingly. "Then we'll prepare the boards," they said.

On the day of the demonstration, however, they brought wooden boards with several large gnarls in the middle, cut into squares no less. What? I asked them where they'd got these boards, and they replied that they had bought it; these extremely cheap woods were just lying around. Those kinds of woods are useless as building materials because they are twisted and gnarled. They're difficult to hammer nails through. That is why they're so cheap. They're not for breaking but for fueling fire. 'Goodness, I didn't think about that. Even preparing a board for breaking is something that needs knowledge!' Sure enough, the demonstration was full of mistakes. The tall adults were kicking and kicking at the boards repeatedly because they couldn't even break one board. Moreover, in breaking, the role of the assistant is more important than that of the kicker. But because they lacked experience, the assistants kept closing their eyes and leaning back whenever a kick flew their way.

To tell the truth, I liked these students but wasn't as comfortable with them as a team. I would give them time to help them, but I found that the team's skills were, frankly, dreadful. Sabrina, who was a 1st degree black belt, would drive two hours every weekend to Nashville, the hometown of country music. She worked as a part-time Taekwondo instructor. But Sabrina was overly proud. Seeing the way she behaved and expected to be treated, one would think she was a Grand Master. She would talk over others and act as a disciplinary captain. Seeing that the members followed me so well, she would even act inappropriately competitive with me. Knowing she couldn't match up to me, one time she called in her dojang instructor, a 2nd-degree black belt, to spar with me. They only lost face. A lot of American dojangs are operated like satellite schools, in which there are several dojangs open here and there, supervised by 1st degree or 2nd degree part-time instructors. In any case, these guys were kicking again and again because they couldn't manage a front kick and back kick properly. As the audience, the elementary school students were just excited and applauded, but I still couldn't help feeling embarrassed that I might be seen as an inadequate instructor.

Finally, it was my turn. I put in extra strength in breaking to make up for the previous mistakes. I demonstrated a breaking where I ran, stepped on the wall then kicked the board. The children raised their hands and asked, "How can you walk on the walls like Spider-man?" It's not much to me, but I guess it looked impressive in the eyes of children who had never seen this kind of demonstration. After kicking, I was to wrap up by finishing with a fingertip thrust breaking. I positioned my finger and looked at the board. I realized that out of all the boards, the assistant was holding up a board with a large gnarl right in the center. 'Argh, can't you guys take a hint? Watch before you pick!' I automatically sighed, thinking of the pain to come to my fingertips. But hundreds of children were looking up at me innocently, and Sabrina was glaring at me in a corner. I didn't have any other choice.

Yelling out kihap, I drive my fingertip in, but only after a long push could I hear a "snap!" sound of the board breaking. The fun of fingertip thrust breaking is that the audience feels the phantom pain and think, 'That must hurt....' I fisted my hand and bowed to the audience before stepping off stage. By then, Sabrina had surrendered completely. I had smashed with my fingertips the board that she couldn't break with her feet. She ran towards me and greeted me with a bow and thanked me for helping. We shook hands, smiling at each other for once.

I opened my fist and showed her my hand. She freaked out seeing my palm soaked with blood. I grinned and said, "Don't try this at home!" It was also a challenge to dare try if she could. 'Do you think being a Master is easy?'

Heading back home, I had to start the car with my left hand. I drove all the way back with one hand. My wife who had been studying greeted me. "How was the demonstration?" "It went well. By the way, can you get me some ice water in a bowl?" Thinking I was going to drink it, my wife brought me a bowl of ice water. I put my hand in, and the water immediately turned red with blood. My wife flipped. "What happened? It's not broken, is it? Didn't I tell you not to do that? Why do you suffer on purpose? Huh? People watching don't even know how hard it is!" Despite my reassurance, my wife burst into tears, while wiping my hand and treating it. If only I could speak English well like Sabrina, I wouldn't have to do things like this as much. 'Ahh, I wonder when I'll be able to speak English properly?'

ATA (American Taekwondo Association)

When my green card came, I decided it was time for me to open my own dojang. However, I didn't know what the legal procedures and processes were, how I should start, what I would need for a contract or anything. I felt uncertain and uneasy, but I didn't have any senior in the United States that I could turn to for advice. A friend who had visited the ATA headquarters told me that if I joined ATA and received instructor training, they would teach me tips for managing an American dojang and provide new techniques. He said that it would lead to success because once I signed up, they would give me frequent consultation and management. My ears opened wide at that. I had learned Taekwondo, but I had no idea how to run a business and what American-style Taekwondo was like.

At that time, the Internet was not widely used and information was dependent on word of mouth. Hearing what my friend who visited ATA had to say, I imagined ATA to be an excellent organization. I made several phone calls and talked to the representative, but despite my curiosity, the information they could provide on the phone was limited. I decided I had to learn the American style properly, and so I dropped everything I was doing to visit the ATA headquarters, located in Little Rock, Arkansas. Once I arrived at the ATA headquarters, I talked to the person in charge and gave a detailed presentation of my needs and experiences. Hearing my introduction, the person in charge replied that at this point they didn't have anything special to teach me. Even their new techniques were things I already knew and wasn't anything I had to learn. They told me that they would contact the big dojangs under ATA so that I could attend the class and learn the know-how from the Masters, and left it at that. In many ways, it wasn't what I was looking for in my situation.

The Rain-Leaking Chickamauga Dojang

In Korea, there are many conditions required to qualify for a dojang. But here, the qualifications of the leading individual didn't matter much. Whatever black belt degree you might be or whether or not you had a license didn't count for very much. As a result, there would sometimes be these ridiculous situations: a student would have fun and feel confident in martial arts and decide to open up a dojang right across the street. They would line up fake trophies in the windows. Well, they were teaching and getting paid as much as their level could, so there's nothing that can be said about their endeavors.

My first dojang opened in Chickamauga, Georgia. It was a historical place, where fierce battles of the Civil War took place and where the Southern Army headquarters had been established. The original name of the city, from the time of the American natives, was still used. Maple leaves would fall on a vast field filled with cannons and monuments. When the sun set, the view would be like a beautiful painting of a landscape. Apart from its history, it was a small town with nothing but a cemetery. It was one of those thoroughly rural villages where there are fewer than twenty shops in the town center. Instead of a proper mat floor tiles, I bought cheap carpets, and I purchased plywood to make my own signboard. People would look in, pass by, but would never sign up. It was a very narrow space. Furthermore, it was at least a 40-minute drive away from home, in a remote location. I didn't have enough money to open a proper dojang anyway, but as this was my first business project, I didn't even know whether it would work or not and, thus, started extremely small.

Soon, a young man came and asked how much it was and what to do to start. I was dismayed. I didn't even know how much I should ask for. In the end, I told him that there were classes five days a week and he could come as much as he wanted, for 50 dollars a month. That's how I got one student to teach. Then one by one, the young people in the town started coming in. The dojang was so narrow that if people stood side by side to do poom-sae, they would kick the wall or kick each other's backside, and students had to maneuver constantly to avoid these obstacles. On rainy days, the roof even leaked. After putting a bucket on the wet carpet, there would be even less room to move around. There was also a pillar in that narrow space that supported the ceiling. It was the worst environment, but everyone still trained enthusiastically.

Chris and Jason, who were the first students to register, were twice my size. Their goal was to lose weight. Training while overcoming the heat awakens people's primitive nature and is especially effective when losing weight. How can you lose weight if you're training in a cool indoors with the air conditioner on? When I explained this, everyone agreed to train without the air conditioner. They trained every day, drenched with sweat in our small and stifling space. Over a summer, they each lost 60 pounds. Their sluggish bodies became sturdy and good-looking. It was a success.

One day, a man who seemed to be in his early thirties came in, with long hair tied back and a handsome mustache. He glared at me. When I asked him how I could help him, he replied that he was Master of a karate school from a neighboring town. He said he'd heard impressive rumors about my skill and had come to participate in class. He spoke as if he was picking a fight. How could he just push open the door and interrupt class like that, without any prior contact? Furthermore, the students saw him and murmured. Apparently, he was well-known in this area for being a karate "world champion." Inwardly I was nervous. 'Is this the kind of thing where they tell you to leave if you lose a fight, the rumored "taking down" your signboard?' He changed into a silk uniform, stood with his black belt and started stretching. Naturally, the students kept looking back and forth between me and the man. His kick that cut the air was sharp, disciplined.

I asked everyone to follow me. Sequence kick, jumping kick, block and kick. A little later the man started huffing and puffing, his disciplined stance gone and lost. He was very different from the world champions that I knew. He panted out that he'd never done these kinds of kicks before, so I asked him where he got his world championship. He said he'd won in a world champion contest organized by their karate association each year at Alabama. So, it wasn't a competition between actual international representatives!

There are many "world champions" like this in America. Some dojangs or other martial arts schools would get together and name themselves World-Something-League, and organize a competition that is a "world competition" only in name. They may call it world championship, but no one from another country ever comes. And so, all the participants become world champions, ranking numbers 1, 2, 3. Male champion, child champion, yellow belt champion, lightweight champion, poom-sae champion, female champion, blue belt champion, board-breaking champion, world champion... So many champions! They then wear a uniform with a large inscription on the back, "2000 Karate World Champion." The "world champion" came in stiff and proud but afterward he bowed and left in a hurry. And he never showed up again. Since then, several people visited the dojang, claiming to be a Master or black belt. But none of them came back a second time.

Teaching Taekwondo with the Whole Body

When I opened my dojang, a lot of fit and energetic young men signed up. They all had excellent strength. I would take their kicks in class. I got knocked down against the wall hundreds of times a day. Each time I would jump up and shout, "Kick harder!" Everyone was amazed at my physical endurance. As a result, however, I would take blows even from inexperienced beginners who would swing their legs around without control. I thought I might end up suffering from a bone disease! I'd instruct them to kick my body, but their feet would come to my face, or I'd tell them to strike at my body, but instead, a punch would hit my head. I once got a bad hit to my mouth and my lips ended up bleeding. "Don't worry," I assured them. "This is nothing to me." And I swallowed the blood pooling inside my mouth. Students would keep on hitting my fingers instead of the target, on the same spot over and over again. My fingers hurt as if they would break. I would have tears in my eyes from pain, but I held it back.

At times, I also had to become a sparring opponent for students. I would narrowly avoid the kicks as they flew past my nose. Because their eyes are not yet fully trained, the students don't know that they've missed. They think they kicked right, but the kick doesn't land. After avoiding their kicks several times, I attack back and kick them hard enough to make them cry. I then growl at the pained students, "I didn't even kick that hard, and you're like that? I guess you'd drop dead if I kicked really hard."

Here, I was no longer an individual. I was representing Korea in this town. My performances showed the standard of Korea. My father was right. "Exalt Korea in the sight of all." A civilian diplomat! I firmly believed that this was another role I had to take up.

The Move to the La Fayette Dojang

A year later, I moved my dojang to the neighboring town. The first dojang was just too narrow and would leak in the rain, so I couldn't stay there any longer. I just wanted a large place to train without any worries, and I found a great location. It was an old and shabby building, but the size was five times bigger than the Chickamauga dojang. Furthermore, one of my parents had told the landlord, "Master Lee is a good and honest man but doesn't have much," so that I was able to get the place at a low price. It was like the workplace of my dreams. I fixed up the place with nails and hammers every day, and finally restarted classes.

However, not long after I reopened my dojang, a young man with messy hair and a shaggy beard started appearing at the dojang. Glaring at the classes through the window, he would stand outside the dojang for ages. He gave me a bad feeling. I had already heard warnings that this town was conservative and very territorial. And, what do you know, it was showing from the very beginning. The man came every day and stared at me from outside the window. 'He'll come in eventually.' The problem was that even if he came in and picked a fight, it wasn't like I could kick him out by beating the crap out of him. Who would send their children to a Master who gets into fistfights with random thugs? Especially when his dojang taught the children respect and discipline. Physical confrontation would be a shortcut to ruining myself. But I was worried because I still had to keep in mind the worst-case scenario.

Then one day, as I was teaching a class, the young man came into the dojang. With an arrogant look in his eyes, he was holding a pole in his hand. My students and their parents, who were waiting for the next class to start, were frightened by this man and his intimidating stance. I went up to him and bowed politely. "How can I help you?" Raising his eyes sharply, he imitated Bruce Lee. (Honestly, I dislike this way of greeting. It is Bruce Lee's way of teaching, to always keep an eye on other people even when saying hello. 'Why do you even bother to say hello, if you can't trust others that much? Just throw a fist first.')

He suddenly started talking about how he had been taught by a renowned Master. He told me the name of his Master and the martial art. It sounded like a Japanese name, and I told him, "My knowledge is limited, and unfortunately I've never heard of him." His face fell. "I'm sorry. I haven't been in the U.S. for that long. Anyway, what's that pole for?" He replied that he brought it here to teach me a lesson. He walked into the middle of the dojang with big strides as if he owned the place, and swung the pole around yelling wildly. I watched him silently. He ran here and there for a while until he was out of breath, still glaring. Each martial artist has his or her pride, but sometimes it becomes too much. These people then tend to think only what they have learned is best and authentic.

I thanked him for his good demonstration skills. "But it's a little different from what I've learned. May I?" I borrowed his pole and spun it around. The pole made air-cutting sounds as I swung it with a force that could knock his head off his shoulders. The young man flinched, and his eyes became that of an abandoned puppy. I gave him back the pole and bowed politely again. Then I told him not to bring these kinds of weapons next time because they could be dangerous. He agreed and bowed, and disappeared with the wind. 'It's always the less trained that go around picking fights, huh.'

I thought that would be the last of him and forgot about the incident. But one day, he appeared again. He barreled towards me in front of other people and put down a bunch of dollar bills. When I asked what this was, he said he was also going to take classes here from now on. I looked at him sharply and told him, "I don't intend to accept you. You're still glaring at me, and your attitude is disrespectful. I'm not a merchant who accepts anyone who pays. If you want to come to our dojang, fix that attitude first!" Nonplussed, he glared at me for a long time, then told me to consider the money as his payment for the class last time. He turned back gruffly. Even at a glance, it looked like several hundred dollars. I called him back. "I'm not interested in this money, so take it back. And don't ever come back again!" He stared at me for a while before eventually picking up the money, and left.

Taekwondo with My Wife

I did a lot of demonstrations during my time in the United States. A demonstration is not something you can do alone. There needs to be at least an assistant or two, though more are better. Moreover, it only works when there is a good dynamic among the Master and assistants. Like other Korean women her age, my wife had always planned to marry after finishing her studies. But after meeting me, she is now a fifth - degree black belt. She went back to Korea and got licensed as an international instructor by Kukkiwon. Others might think that she reached fifth degree easily as the wife of a Taekwondo Master, but it is not so. It's difficult to reprimand adult trainees when teaching them. But from time to time, the Master's wife would be scolded terribly. "Is that how I taught you? Is that all you can do?" Seeing my wife standing in attention stance and being scolded sharply by me in class, other students and parents would nervously hold their breath. Even when she teared up, there was no exception. I reprimanded her even harder for crying. I taught her strictly. They say married couples get divorced even because of driving lessons! But the Taekwondo my wife learned through her tears is incredible. So, most board breaking or self-defense demonstrations are possible even just with the two of us present.

My wife was fragile when we first got married. To keep up with her classes in English, she had to work twice or three times as much as others. With all her energy used up, she would collapse whenever she came back from school. I trained her Taekwondo because I thought that the exercise would help her to gain physical strength and allow her to concentrate better. She followed without complaint and ended up very healthy. Instead of sitting at the table all day, she also took time to let her body perspire and consequently both her mind and body became brighter and happier. Her docile and introverted personality turned more vibrant and outgoing. I always hesitate when someone asks me if Taekwondo is good for your body. I know from experience that it may not always be the case. All the broken parts of my body were injuries from Taekwondo. So, I couldn't say it was always so. However, my wife confidently told people that Taekwondo was good. And because she was living proof, her words had power.

When the students arrive before class time, she comes out to practice poom-sae with them. From my childhood to my time as a military instructor, I tediously practiced the poom-sae thousands and thousands of times. So, I could never enjoy poom-sae. However, my wife likes it because she says it's an excellent exercise that makes you sweat thoroughly if you do it right. I tell her that there are so many things you can do other than poom-sae, but my wife insists on practicing her poom-sae with a passion. I can't even begin talking about how helpful she is in class. I just teach and talk in the front, but my wife helps students who don't have partners by being their opponent. She runs together with them as partners, whether they are children or adults. She is someone who thoroughly enjoys Taekwondo. She makes time in her busy schedule to come to the dojang and tells me to relax while she's there. Then she takes care of stretching exercises, teaching poom-sae, counseling, and even class registration. The things I do with difficulty, she does happily. It becomes hard for me to be at the dojang by myself whenever my wife is away.

My wife is also a senior member of our demonstration team. She is a small woman, but when you see her rolling forward on the mat-less concrete ground or yelling out kihap while swinging her nun-chucks, or kicking and breaking, she looks so bold. That is why even though my wife is always kind and smiling, no one treats her with condescension.

She also loves demonstrating self-defense with me. I always play the pathetic villain, and my wife easily defeats me with her short but fast arms and legs, then poses in front of the audience and grins. The audience loves it. She is a different person on stage. Her kihap is strong and the very look in her eyes changes. She really knows how to enjoy a demonstration. It is both rewarding and fun to demonstrate together. In front of others, we pretend to be invincible. Then we come back home and struggle and laugh as we apply medicine to each other. My wife is my best friend in the whole world. And my wife became the person who understands me best, thanks to Taekwondo.

My Wife Rises Up

My wife graduated from university and entered graduate school. The campus was picturesque with a 150-year-old history and the nickname "The Oxford of the South." She was the only Asian student enrolled in the graduate program. Not only was it difficult to get in, but the expensive tuition also wasn't something I could afford. My wife was offered a full scholarship. I was so grateful and proud. But the reality was that everything was a challenge. The English used in graduate school seemed to be a language on a whole other level.

She had to read enormous amounts of books and frequently write essays, and this wasn't something that I could help her with. Moreover, each class was full of passionate debates that she could barely participate in. Students would have heated discussions among themselves. She told me how they wouldn't even let her join, as if she was invisible. Struggling and crying, she finished a whole semester like that.

There was a dinner party at the end of the first semester, in which students could bring family. It was my first time attending a dinner party in the United States and I was extremely nervous. My wife and I attended the party wearing hanbok. In her hanbok, people started looking at her differently and, for once, initiated conversation with her. While talking to the dean, I told him that I teach Taekwondo, and he suggested in passing that it would be nice if I could show them something. It felt like a great opportunity. "OK!" I replied and immediately brought breaking boards from my car.

In the party room that was beautifully lit by the fireplace, we gave an impromptu demonstration. Of course, I put my wife as much in the spotlight as possible. I had my wife break various boards. Unlike her usual quiet demeanor, she showed a fierceness in her eyes. The thick boards were totally shattered by those small hands and feet! Eyes widened. I picked people from the audience and asked them to hold up three balloons in the air. Everyone seemed to wonder what would happen. My wife held up her long skirts with both hands and yelling out a long kihap. She ran, jumped in the air and burst all three balloons in a second, before landing on the floor gracefully. Everyone was amazed. The usually unnoticeable petite female Asian student was then flying in the air with her skirts hitched up in front of all the students, professors, and even their families. Her eyes were sharp, her kihap loud, and her smile proud, all while she was grabbing and throwing me with speed and skill. Everyone's mouth was agape. The demonstration ended with a standing ovation from the audience. My wife modestly bowed. The dean and his wife came over, shook hands with my wife and sang her praises. He told us how he had no idea that the only Asian female student at their graduate school had such impressive skills, and that he would love to learn, too. The other professors and students gathered around as well, wanting to take pictures together with her. It was the moment where the foreigner became the hero.

After that, I cannot say enough how nice her fellow graduate students were to my wife. They would happily help her with anything, like writing her thesis or debating. They would invite her to all kinds of extracurricular activities, wanting to hang out together even on weekends. A friend who was an air-force pilot even took us on a flight, offering to teach us how to fly a plane. As everyone became close friends, my wife also started enjoying school and attended class with a smile on her face. Our dojang demonstration team was also invited to perform at an event at her graduate school. My students and their families learned that my wife was studying for a master's degree in a university where even Americans had difficulty getting accepted. Thanks to that realization, they not only looked at my wife but also me, with new eyes. 'It's just that they're a little poor at speaking English, but they're not uneducated people at all!'

I cannot say enough about all the help she received until her graduation. Her friends and her professors loved my wife and considered her an extraordinary friend. Even when my wife applied for her doctorate, the professor who interviewed her said that he had never seen anyone receive such good recommendation letters. All of this was thanks to the impromptu Taekwondo demonstration that day. So, no wonder my wife loves Taekwondo even more than I do. Thanks to Taekwondo, my wife rose up!

The Police Want Hands-On Experience

Americans working in professional jobs have a very keen sense of professionalism. And amongst professional people, I cannot say enough about police officers. They are all very tough guys. The American police are especially intimately exposed to gunfights. Shootings are somewhat frequent as most criminals have access to guns. Furthermore, in a gunfight, it is not easy to identify who is an assailant and who is not. Naturally, these people have to be very sharp and sensitive to their surroundings.

Doug, a police officer whom I taught, had a scar from a gunshot wound on his upper chest, right below his neck. Out of all places, he had gotten hit right above his bulletproof vest. He had literally come back from the dead. A colleague of his had been shot through from the sides, right above his vest towards his armpit and had died on the spot. A bulletproof vest does not guarantee survival. So, in a dangerous situation, they must fight for their lives. These occupations give people a particular interest in self-defense. The police regulations allow the police to catch a criminal for arrest, but do not let them punch or kick the criminal to catch him or her. However, laws aside, in a life-threatening situation, one must always be mindful of a second or third weapon. Therefore, these policemen usually have another gun hidden in their bodies. Their shooting skills are also excellent.

Most men in my neighborhood would keep knives in their pockets.

Knives, even if they look threatening, do not register as a lethal weapon if they are less than 4-inch long. The children here sometimes are given knives or guns as Christmas or birthday presents. Living in an environment naturally exposed to weapons, people treat small knives as mere convenient tools. Because they live a life always exposed to guns and knives, the police officers I have met were genuinely interested in self-defense against these weapons. Teaching them these things, you get recognized as a competent Master.

One day, Doug came into the dojang with an excited expression. He had visited the prison earlier when a criminal who he had caught recognized him. The criminal came up to him to pick a fight. When Doug warned him to keep back, that he'd learned Taekwondo, the criminal demanded what use would that be, and attempted to attack him. Remembering the self-defense that he had learned, he twisted the opponent's wrist – which ended up turning 180 degrees. I was taken aback. To twist someone's wrist to that extent, even if he was under attack! But according to Doug, in the case that prisoners attack the guards or the police, it could turn into a life-or-death situation. It is not a situation where they can go easy on the prisoners. I asked him to present his experience to the class. The police officer enthusiastically told the class he had used a technique that we had learned the day before and testified that the self-defense technique was genuinely useful. You can imagine how eager and excited the class was that day.

I once held a self-defense seminar for local police officers, partially also to promote the dojang. Quite a few police officers attended. I taught them simple falling techniques, breaking techniques, and punching techniques, among others, and everyone followed well, sweaty and enthusiastic. I created self-defense role-play situations. Scenarios like when the opponent pulls out the gun before me, or when the opponent tries to get ahold of my weapon, etc. I showed them short but powerful techniques that could be useful in such situations.

A police officer on patrol then came in, wearing his uniform. He said he wanted to join but that he was on duty, and couldn't take off his shoes. I said that I would go out to teach him outside the mat. I left the mat and told him to point his gun towards me. Immediately after the words left my mouth, he pulled out his pistol from his sides, removed the magazine and held it against my face. It suddenly turned into a real situation. The person holding the pistol and the spectators were all police officers. Everyone looked on curiously.

In the movies, villains usually shoot carelessly with the gun in one hand. But that is never the case with professionals with real jobs that require shooting. These people hold their pistols tightly with both hands. In a real situation, they would put some distance between themselves and the opponent to prevent being jumped on. Unfortunately, the distance between myself and the officer was too close. Stepping sideways, I strike his wrists with my knife hand like a pair of scissors and held both his arms in place with my armpits. Then I put my entire body weight on his gun arm and twisted it away, keeping the gunpoint towards the sky. But the police officer refused to drop the gun and resisted actively. I couldn't take it easy at that point, because if I lost, my lessons would lose credibility. It was a battle for pride, between a police officer and a Taekwondo master. We wrestled on the ground for a while until I twisted his arm backward, and finally, he said, "OK! I yield!" Then everyone clapped thunderously. The police officer commented how his twisted arm and wrists were aching. Afterward, at town festivals, officers on patrol duty would say hello first. I was grateful that I seemed to have gained some public acknowledgement.

Sometimes they would turn up with a surprise test for me. They would tell me of a difficult problem and ask me to solve it. If I could not come up with a convincing answer as soon as they ask the question, I would lose face. Because if I couldn't solve it on the spot, would there be no way out in a real situation?

Phillip was also a policeman. He once told me how he had grappled with a 300-pound man, as he tried to arrest him, but was pinned to the ground. He was running out of strength and had let go of his gun.

Fortunately, his colleague ran over and saved him, but he almost died of fright, thinking that the criminal might get ahold of his gun. "Master Lee, what would you do? However, as a rule, you can't strike him." And that's how it goes. If you can think of a short and clear answer, the higher chance you have surviving in the United States as a Taekwondo master. Of course, I came up with an answer that had Phillip exclaim, "Aha!"

Promotion Test

It usually takes three years of training to become a 1st-degree black belt. Some dojangs take up to 4 or 5 years. If you fall short of any required criteria, then you are disqualified from the test. Therefore, a "black belt" is recognized as someone with a high level of self-discipline. The test itself is not easy either. It is a place and moment where you must show everything you have learned in the past.

My dojang's black belt promotion test also focuses on demonstrating what the student has learned over the past three years to prove his or her worth, in the presence of witnesses. The invited family members and friends come knowing that the student had been learning Taekwondo but surprised at how much he or she has learned, and awed as they watch the student pass the difficult tests, one by one. No matter the age of a student, you cannot help but feel deep respect for them. And through this test process, the student experiences self-achievement and gains confidence.

The main presentations of the test consist of physical strength and basic form, kicking, sparring, one-step sparring, self-defense, breaking, answering questions regarding Taekwondo, and so on. Additional presentations may be added depending on the dojang. The 1st-degree promotion test is like this, and the 2nd degree and 3rd degree promotion test, of course, becomes even more difficult.

In the case of our dojang, we place considerably more importance on breaking than other techniques. The 1st degree must break 30 boards and one 2-inch thick cement block, while the 2nd degree must break 50 boards and two cement blocks. The 3rd-degree black belt must break 100 boards and three cement blocks with his or her knife hand all at once. Although it looks tough, I readjust the level of difficulty by taking the student's ability into consideration, so he or she will only feel a slight ache in his or her hands and feet. It is so that I may help the student to show everything he or she has learned so far in front of families and relatives. Every time a board breaks the audience claps and cheers.

In the last breaking, the student must break the cement block by striking it with a hand. This is the biggest hurdle. It can also be a significant burden to smaller or female students. When it doesn't break even after striking and striking, I become as anxious with the families watching. I pray that they will break it without getting hurt. Female students sometimes cry because of the pain in their hands or the fear of being unable to break the block. But there are no exceptions. That is why I have them train in a breaking exercise, months before the test for this moment. The students collect broken pieces of boards from previous promotion tests and reuse them by breaking the boards again, striking across the grain at a straight angle. Not only with your hands hurt from the exercise, but you will need several times more force to accomplish it. A few hundred breaking practices will give you the strength and the know-how. Confidence that you have prepared a long time for this moment is notably the most crucial factor. Because at any rate, that moment is a moment of battle with yourself. Neither your parents nor friends can help. Furthermore, the silent audience's eyes and my—the judge's—eyes act as additional pressure. You control your mind and focus, and with a sudden loud kihap, you strike down with all your power. When the block finally crashes down with a "wham," the audience bursts into enthusiastic cheers and the parents have tears in their eyes. The student feels so proud of his or her achievement.

Lastly, there is blowing out candles with a fist. You must extinguish three candles in a row. It is a simple test, but a challenge nonetheless. You would like to put them all out at once, like the Master, but that is not easy to do when you are already exhausted. Watching the student wrestle with the candle that refuses to extinguish, it is the audience that grows more desperate. But heaven helps those who help themselves; when the candles go out, and its lights disappear, the joy doubles. The judge, the Master, the families, relatives, and friends all become united in their joy. It is because solidarity becomes deeper when people go through difficult things together. I believe that in these moments, people are reborn. They break their small selves and grow into bigger selves.

Upon the completion of the test, I immediately announce the student's promotion and award the black belt. It gives the student closure in the culmination of his or her long journey and allows them to take the first steps into their next adventure.

After awarding the black belt, I conduct a tea ceremony to share tea. It is like a sacrament. My wife and I sit behind a nice table and place a teacup on top. There is Korean traditional music playing in the background.

The new black belt students bow deeply as we pour tea for them to drink, and they reciprocate. Then they do it again, which I return with a respectful nod of my head. Next, we have parents and grandparents sit in front of the students. The students kneel, bow down their heads deeply, and present the tea. Receiving the bowl and the cup of tea that their children respectfully offer them with both hands, none of the parents can help but shed tears. I explain to them that this is a show of gratitude for raising them, and of promise that they will be a better son or daughter. And so, the bond between parents and their children becomes stronger than ever.

When all is done, everyone shares the food that the families have prepared. It is a treat for the guests who have watched and encouraged the students throughout the test. When you spread out the cookies and cakes and other homemade food, it is as good as any party. The students chat animatedly about Taekwondo, as they look back on their mistakes during the test with laughter and show off their red and raw hands and feet. They praise and congratulate each other and take photos together while the excitement is still fresh. This moment remains forever in their minds as a happy and memorable experience. My dojang's black belt promotion test is organized like a small festival so that the students become the stars of the day. The black belt is a valuable medal only for those who have won the battle against themselves through their honest efforts.

Karate? Taekwondo?

Among people to visit the dojang for the first time, there were some who said that they have learned martial art before. They would tell me its name, but I couldn't understand. I would ask them how to write the name, and they would spell out "karate." "Oh, karate!" Americans usually can't pronounce the word "karate" properly. Furthermore, some tend to think that all martial arts are karate. New students would come into the dojang and say that they came to learn karate. I tell them that I teach Taekwondo. I would explain that karate is a Japanese martial art, kungfu is a Chinese martial art, while Taekwondo is a martial art that originates from Korea. A lot of American dojangs still have big signboards that say 'karate,' even though they hang up a Korean flag indoors. I also was torn when I first opened my dojang. I was worried that people wouldn't know what we did, due to the unfamiliarity of the word "Taekwondo." In the end, I still wrote "Taekwondo" on my signboard. Even if it made things more difficult, I felt I had to keep our true identity.

The United States is commonly called "the Melting Pot." It is a country where various cultures and races coexist. As such, martial arts and sects from all over the world also coexist. Different martial arts are introduced and naturally combined inside the dojangs. They write 'karate' on the signboard while putting up the Korean national flag inside the dojang, or advertise on the windows that they teach Hapkido, Kungfu,

Kickboxing, Muaythai, Yoga, Jiujitsu, Kendo, Taichi, and all other martial arts.

Seeing these, my students asked why I only taught Taekwondo. Do I not know any other martial arts? I answered, "Each martial art has its strong points. Taekwondo is advantageous in that its kicks are brilliant, fast, and strong. You also can learn techniques like twisting and throwing—that are strong points in other martial arts—as much as you would need to through Taekwondo training, so don't worry." Students believe that Masters are Masters of all martial arts. In other words, they see Masters as experts on all sides of martial arts. Many students have learned other martial arts before coming to a Taekwondo dojang. Therefore, one should not have a narrow-minded prejudice against other martial arts.

The art of weaponry is both flamboyant and entertaining. It is therefore natural to be attracted to it. There is a saying, "all weapons sprout from bare hands." Barehanded martial arts give rise to weapon-based martial arts. That is why even ancient martial artists would train in both. I tell my students that if I hold a weapon while doing Taekwondo techniques, immediately that becomes a form of simple weapon-based martial art. If I held up a sword and practiced low block, middle block, and high block, then strike, block, strike, or poom-sae, then that in itself would be weapons training. That is why I also teach basic swordsmanship, and the arts of spears, nun-chucks, ninja throwing stars, and even knife throwing for fun.

Most martial arts teach the culture of their origin. Chinese martial arts are taught wearing Chinese uniforms, with Chinese etiquette and terminology. Japanese martial arts are also taught and learned in Japanese style. So, Taekwondo is taught along with Korean culture.

As a result, students naturally come to respect and love the birthplace of martial art in which they train. They become interested in the culture, the ideas, and the languages of that country. Students who love Taekwondo often choose Korean products, if the price is about the same. I would like to say that Taekwondo and its instructors have had a hidden hand in creating the new Korean wave in the United States for Korean companies such as Samsung, LG, Kia, and Hyundai.

Some consider Korea to be the home of the mind, somewhere they want to visit once in their lifetime. It is an unknown country that has just begun to spread its wings, after its long and ancient silence. As such, people feel thankful for their precious bonds with Masters who have flown across the Pacific. To keep up with these students' expectations, we must have Taekwondo become something beyond a sport—it has to be a road to improving one's mind.

Seizure Kick

My English was weak, but I still had to teach. Sometimes if I felt impatient, I would blurt things out in Korean. I was ever so grateful to my students, who despite this, followed my instructions intuitively. Taekwondo is something your body can learn by following repetitively the movements of the instructor. When the teacher and the student connect through their minds, words become less important. Therefore, Taekwondo can be taught and learned without having to speak fluently. Of course, studying English was still essential, since as a Master, I also had to teach students thoughts and ideas of the mind.

There is a technique named "scissor kick," in which you kick with your legs like a scissor. But the pronunciation wasn't easy for me. I would teach my students to scissor kick, but they would be utterly terrible at it. "Kick straight, like a scissor." They would reply diligently, "Yes, sir!" and enthusiastically continue their sloppy kicks. A few years passed like that. One day a student asked me why the kick was named as such. "What about it? Scissor kick." The student made a scissoring motion with his hands and asked if I was talking about this kind of scissors. "That's what I said. Scissor!"

Everyone burst out laughing. Apparently, I had been pronouncing the word as "seizure" for years. I guess that was why their scissor kicks looked like they were having seizures. No matter how much I listened and repeated them, both words sounded the same to me. Aside from that, people wouldn't ask questions even if they didn't understand something due to my poor pronunciation or grammar. When I belatedly asked them why they always answered "Yes, sir!" without understanding, the students replied that they thought it was an absolute rule to answer that way. They also thought I was speaking some Taekwondo jargon. What other occupation would allow you to work confidently in the United States with such poor English?

Defeating Tough Guys

Sometimes students ask, "Does Master Lee have any experience with street fighting?" Of course, I have. There have been many incidents during my childhood where I had to beat up bullies that tormented the weak. When I told them stories of saving girls from molesters in the streets at night, people would listen in wonder, as if I were telling them a heroic epic. Stories that are nothing special in Korea become exciting real-life accounts for people who want to know if Taekwondo can be used in real life. Because of strict laws, fist fighting in the streets is not as common in the United States as it is in Korea. So, people hardly ever see or experience street fighting. Because of this, civilians have no idea what to do in fights and even fear them. Thus, they think that people who have experience in reckless fighting must be great fighters.

One day, I received a phone call. The caller spoke abruptly, with a blunt southern accent, clearly a "tough guy." He said he was going to enter a UFC competition, and had learned all the martial arts that he needed fighting. He just wanted to strengthen his kicking skills a little. He asked if I could teach him. I answered that I couldn't say over the phone and suggested that he come visit my school first.

The next day, a white man in his late twenties walked in. He was tall, with a shaved head. He was wearing a short-sleeved shirt and short pants, and I could see his muscular form and impressive tattoos all over his body. He looked like the stereotypical street fighter. But his eyes were very arrogant and vicious. Even at a glance, it was clear that he had not come here to learn anything.

He abruptly started telling me how he was going to enter a UFC preliminary two months later, and that he wanted to do some intense work out until then. There was an MMA (Mixed Martial Arts) gym in another neighborhood that he practiced at with his friends, but he had wanted to get extra training at a nearer location and had decided to visit us. He continued to list the names of all kinds of martial arts. From what he told me, he had never actually trained in any of them until the end, and had jumped here and there like a grasshopper, only learning techniques that might help in fights. Therefore, he wasn't someone who would patiently learn from me either.

"You have any adults here that I might spar with? What's your specialty? They say you're tough, is that true? You have anything you might be able to teach me?" It was apparent that he would go around beating up my students and eventually challenge me, too.

The man had also brought his 6-year-old son, and bragged about how his kid was skilled in fighting like his father and how he had beaten up all his peers. "Is that so? I can't put you with my regular students, but I can do a 1-to-1 private lesson." That's precisely what he wanted, he declared. He said that we should start immediately and asked for the price. "I'm $250 per hour. If you're interested, we can start now." He hesitated. "$250?" The minimum wage in Georgia in 2012 was less than $7.50 per hour.

I asked with a stern face, "Do you think I'm an amateur?" He said no. "You're right. I'm a professional. In the time that I teach you, I could be teaching 30 people. You'll have to compensate me for that time." And at once, the man's arrogance was gone.

"What do you do for a living?" He told me that he goes around fighting while his wife supports the family. I asked him how much he earns each match, and he said he would earn $70 in a preliminary round. Then the more you win, the more the award money you would receive—$100 more, then $200 more. But in a regional competition like that, the hospital bills could cost more than that. The "tough guy" left, dejected, muttering about how professionals were, indeed, different.

Traveling the World with Taekwondo

Even now, many Americans are born, raised, and die in the state of their birth. The people in this town were people who even regarded Atlanta, a city only about two hours away, as a foreign land. They didn't like the traffic jams or the proximity of houses in the big cities. Thus, big cities such as New York, Los Angeles or Chicago were places to be seen in movies or on TV, but never in real life.

I wanted to build a bridge of communication between the outside world and the young people from our dojang. I deliberately took the opportunity to go to demonstrations all over the place. From nearby Atlanta, we traveled farther. In the west, we visited California, Utah, Arizona, while in the north we even passed the Niagara Falls and crossed the Canadian border. My students were able to see a little more of the world than their peers. American students would follow my wife and me around like baby ducklings, getting onto planes, taxis, and buses for the first time. It must have been an amusing scene to onlookers.

I previously mentioned a dojang in Little Tokyo, Los Angeles that I visited during my first visit to America in 1995. It was the dojang of the action actors, Grand Master Jun Chong of Ninja Turf and Master Phillip Rhee of Best of the Best. Ten years later, I visited again with my students. Luckily, we visited on the one day of the week that Master Phillip Rhee came in to teach. Thanks to that, we had the opportunity to meet both Grand Master Jun Chong and Master Phillip Rhee. My students were excited to be able to visit a dojang that actual movie action actors were running. Master Phillip Rhee took one look at me and said that I looked familiar. My students who were looking at the photos on the wall found my face in one of them and pointed it out. "Isn't that Master Lee?"

I told him that I had visited this dojang ten years ago with a demonstration team and that I was in the corner of that photo on the wall. Master Phillip Rhee replied that he had been curious about this photo for a long time. Traditionally, the dojang had never put up pictures of anyone uninvolved with their dojang, yet when he came back from a trip to Korea in 1995 to advertise his film, he surprisingly found an unfamiliar face on the wall. My students could barely contain their excitement. Not only was their Master standing side by side with an action movie star, laughing and talking, but his face was also hung up on the movie star's dojang's wall!

We received a videotape starring Grand Master Jun Chong with his handwritten autograph as a gift. We even had the opportunity to be invited on the spot to participate in a class taught by Master Phillip Rhee himself. And as expected of Master Phillip Rhee, his charisma was evident even in his class. The kicks and punches that he first-handedly demonstrated cut the air with a speed of the wind. Exclamations of awe came out of our mouths. His skills from the movie were by no means exaggerated.

I also brought my students to Korea. From the colorful streets of nighttime Seoul to famous scenic spots with thousands of years of history, I showed them all around the country. My students were genuinely impressed by the coexistence of modernity and tradition.

"Master Lee, Korea is so small on the map, but why is the city so big? Why doesn't it end?" The endless forest of buildings must have been fascinating. "Wow, the floor is so warm!" They exclaimed, putting their faces down on the floor with a heating system. I was at first worried that Korean food may not be to their taste, but my students loved street foods like kimbap (seaweed-wrapped rice and other ingredients cut into bite-sized pieces), spicy rice cake, fish cake, and fried dishes. Holding and chewing grilled squid, they walked along the streets. They completely fell in love with the taste of squid, to the point that when we came back, they would turn up to the dojang chewing grilled squid. They would go out of their way to visit a faraway Korean food store to buy it. They would reprimand their friends for their fear of the unknown food. "They don't know how delicious this is, poor things!" The Korea that they had seen was a land of wonder and miracles that created from a brilliant culture and civilization.

Although we wandered around the world whenever we had the chance, the most foreign place we visited for demonstrations was none other than the local nursing home. I frequently went to demonstrate at nursing homes. They were the first place I would go after forming a demonstration team each year. Nursing homes do not get a lot of visitors, so they welcome anyone who visits. I was able to teach the students to do their best even in a small place and teach them to share and spread love through Taekwondo.

At nursing homes, as the senior citizens sit in wheelchairs, they look out and live by the window and wait all day for someone who never comes. So, when children and young people around the age of their grandchildren visit to demonstrate, they all come out in their wheelchairs and with their oxygen tanks. Some elders who cannot sit up even come out in their wheeled beds to watch. They are so happy to see small children doing their best. Hearing young people's strong kihap gives them the strength that they didn't remember they had and makes them clench their fists in excitement.

Although not at first, their younger relatives slowly visit less and less, too busy living in the outside world. They barely visit once or twice during the holidays. Many elders do not get visitors for a year or two because their children have moved to other states for their jobs. Lying in a hospital-like room where only nurses wearing uniforms come and go, people become homesick and confused after a year.

Cut off from the outside world and its people, these residents inhabit a land of hopelessness where they can only wait for their dying day. That is why the elders are delighted whenever anyone visits. For someone visiting for the first time, the repellent smell in cheap nursing homes makes it hard to breathe. A gray shadow of death overshadows the place. Children and young people are reluctant to visit. And yet, this is the place where one can truly learn the meaning of life.

After the demonstration, I have the members walk up to each grandfather and grandmother, hold their hands, and ask if they enjoyed the demonstration. The elders are moved to tears. The moment that young and adorable children hold their pale and dry hands, they become so blissful. Humans are beings that live off love and attention.

Some people are lying in bed with a respirator over their faces. You can see their clouded eyes losing focus. They can't even speak, so they show their gratitude through their teary eyes. Their hands are impossibly cold. You feel solemn, looking at how the warmth of life seems to be fading away from them. They ask us to visit again next time, unable to let go of our hands. We swear that we will come back, but even then, we cannot promise that we will see them again, because they may not wait for us. Leaving the nursing homes, waving at the old men and women hanging behind the windows, the children also seem to feel something unspeakable. A place where Death visits more than lively young people, it is the last station of life. It is the closest yet farthest place, the forgotten end of the world.

The L.A. Madman

On the last day of the pleasant trip, we were riding a bus in L.A with joy, passing through the streets I had seen in movies. At one station, a burly man got on the bus, shouting and cursing and threatening people as if he would bite. 'Is he crazy? Did he take drugs?"

As the man roughly pushed through towards the back seats, the frightened passengers rushed to the front of the bus. Only our group was left in the back compartment. And wouldn't you know, the man squeezed in and dropped into the middle of the rear seat, where our dojang's young students were sitting. Everyone scooted closer to the window, looking at me from the side of his or her eyes.

I tried to think of a plan in case of an emergency, but I was at loss as to what to regarding 'self-defense against a madman'. Reluctantly, I planned to strike first if anything were to happen. I did not want to cause trouble, but should I not protect the students I led first and foremost?

Even sitting down, the man continued, "President Bush kidnapped me through the FBI, tortured me, and planted a bug in my ear! I hear messages of space! The world is ruined! What are you looking at? I'll kill you all!" Then he took out odds and ends from his bag and his pockets, throwing them at people, but no one could stop him.

Meanwhile, a coin fell from the man's pocket, rolled away and stopped. Suddenly, an unexpected situation occurred. It was my wife. She abruptly stood up from her seat, picked up the coin and marched towards the man. Then she put her hands together right in front of his face and clapped loudly, "clap, clap!" All the bus passengers and the madman alike widened their eyes in surprise.

"Sir, you dropped a coin here!" And then, "Stop yelling. No one can understand what you're saying." My wife's unexpected behavior not only had me at loss for words but also rendered the madman speechless. "Where did you come from? What's your name? Whom did you say tortured you?" At once, the bus fell silent.

It was clear to see the man felt absurd, facing a small Asian woman, whose full height was only about his sitting height, fearlessly asking this and that. So, did I. 'What is this situation? Should I stop her or not?'

As my wife's inquisitive questions continued, the glaring man reluctantly started answering one by one, then gradually begin to become docile as a tamed lion before its trainer. Like pouring water on a red-hot iron stick, 'Pshhh~!' he deflated, and his voice turned low, and his surly face gradually turned into a that of a well-groomed young man. I had no idea a that such a rough-looking face could change so quickly.

Although his conversation with my wife was a little incoherent, it was interesting to listen to him because his answers to the questions stood out so vividly. As the mood gradually softened, even our dojang's young people sat around one by one and joined the conversation. The bus driver and passengers were stealing glances with surprised eyes at the suddenly reversed situation, especially as the conversation started making sense and there were peals of laughter.

After a fascinating conversation, we arrived at our destination. He even politely shook our hands, and said, "You are unlike other people. You have ears that listen. You are good people. Have a good travel."

The bus left in an asymmetrical population distribution, the front compartment packed tightly with standing passengers and the empty back compartment with the man sitting alone, his both legs stretched out. One of our female students suddenly burst out laughing. She said she had been so scared that she couldn't even breathe, and then thought she would faint from my wife's sudden and daring behavior. She said that she could only shout inwardly, 'Oh, no, please!'

My wife is always calm in these situations. When things become urgent, I think about using my fist beforehand, but my wife always resolves the situation with words. Now that I think about it, my wife had really made up her mind to sincerely listen to the words of that raving man. She had listened wholeheartedly to the words of the man who was running amuck with a fire in his chest for whatever reason. It seems that this had evaporated his Fire Energy and calmed him down as if a charcoal fire had been removed from his chest.

Doctor Aaron, Thrown Over

Amongst my students was Doctor Aaron. He was a handsome and tall man, with a well-built physique. Everyone liked him. He worked out regularly and had strong muscles to show it. He told me that he had done wrestling and footfall during his school days. He had done everything but Taekwondo. He also had great concentration, so his skills increased steadily and quickly. Despite everything, however, I had some difficulty teaching him. When I showed him a technique, he would persistently ask the principles behind it. He was a highly intelligent and curious person, so I could not answer him half-heartedly. He would study the essential points of each move and ask how it worked, what the difference between fist fighting and Taekwondo was, along with many other questions.

He seemed to think that there was a mysterious principle behind Taekwondo or Eastern martial arts that was unknown to him. However, it was difficult for me to answer when he asked about the physical body. Even if I knew, how could my knowledge in that area compare to a doctor's? In addition, he trained hard. It hurt to receive his kicks.

Then, the incident happened. I was demonstrating self-defense in which I flipped my opponent by pulling at his neck, when he raised his hands to ask a question. "What if your opponent doesn't go along with the technique like now, and forcibly stand his ground?" Other students would easily nod and say, "Oh, I see," but Doctor Aaron was different.

He suggested that I try to flip him over while he stood his ground. Everyone looked between him and me. 'Ugh, I knew this would happen someday.' I faced him reluctantly. When I grabbed his neck and pulled, he pushed his lower body backward and didn't budge.

Doctor Aaron was standing ground with all his strength. That was his weak point. I pulled his right leg with my left hand and pushed his shoulder sharply away. Doctor Aaron flipped over backward. He then suddenly screamed and rolled over, his face turned white. He couldn't even breathe properly from the pain. "Doctor Aaron, what's wrong? You're a doctor, tell me what is wrong!" He replied that his knee hurt so much. I wrapped an ice pack around his knee with a towel and immediately called his wife. His wife, who was exercising at the fitness center across the street, hurriedly ran over and transferred him to hospital.

There is nothing more worrisome than one of my students getting injured during class. I would rather have myself injured—watching someone get hurt and carried away shortens my lifespan.

A few days later, Doctor Aaron came to see me on crutches with a bandage around his leg. He had had surgery from severed knee ligament. He apologized, saying he wouldn't be able to do Taekwondo anymore. When I apologized fervently back, he replied that I shouldn't be sorry about anything. He laughed, saying that it was his fault for challenging Master Lee. Doctor Aaron's hospital was one of the best in our town. When patients went to see the doctor and saw him wearing a cast on his leg, they would ask what on earth happened. Doctor Aaron would reply that he'd lost to Master Lee. Rumor ran fast in the small town. "The Taekwondo Master beat up the tall and handsome doctor."

Power Breaking and Internal Injury

In elementary school, my teacher told me that you had to break your limbs several times to become a Taekwondo Master. Intimidated, I remember thinking that I could never be a Master. But I did become a Master and looking back, his words were very accurate. I did frequently break my limbs.

As a Korean Master with poor English, I showed a lot of power breaking to avoid being looked down upon. I found materials for breaking in various household goods. Things I saw daily around me were practical because I knew their solidity. In my free time, I would visit building material stores and look around for anything new. When I would come out with only a few bricks, a clerk who loved joking would strike up a conversation with me. "What'll you build with so little bricks? A house?" Then I would reply without thinking, "No, I'm going to kick them with my feet." "What?" His eyes would go around. And I would say, "It's just a hobby."

Sometimes I kick and break cement blocks instead of wooden boards. You must look carefully at the materials before choosing them. The materials are all different depending on what store you visit. Once, I demonstrated a back kick as usual. I kicked the block but felt a tremendous impact, and my heel felt like it was shattering. My feet felt so hot and burnt—I could almost feel smoke rising from the sole of my foot. With each step I walked, I choked and winced with the pain cutting through my bones. My swollen ankle looked like I had broken my heel bones. 'What on earth? It never hurt like this before!' Later on, I found that the block wasn't the cement block that I usually used, but one with gravel! Concrete blocks are much heavier and sturdier with the gravel embedded in them. The colors and shapes might be similar, but the difference in their solidity is vastly different. At first, I had much difficulty in telling the difference between them, and my limbs suffered greatly for it.

When I visit a building material store and ask for 2-inch thick blocks, people I don't even know ask, "Are you Master Lee?" They tell me they've heard that I break blocks with my bare hands, and ask if I've come to buy blocks for that. When I answer yes, they shake hands with me. "Even the energy in your hands is different." "My hands are numb from shaking yours." They say all sorts of things. I just smile at them.

The Broken Baseball Bats

There was another "tough guy" who frequently taunted me. He would show off that he used to be in Special Forces and flaunt his toughness. Every word and action said, "A Taekwondo Master? So, what?" Naturally, I didn't feel very comfortable around him. One day, I was performing a demonstration and saw him among the audience. I called him out since I needed someone with a strong grip. He agreed and stepped up. I told him he just needed to hold on tightly to the bat as if he was batting. He wasn't thinking much of it until I kicked the bat with a spin hook kick. My heel hit the bat, and it broke and flew off with a loud 'crack!'. His jaw fell open. Holding the bat, he would have felt the impact as the bat broke off with his hands. His attitude changed at once. "It really broke. Wow! I see Taekwondo in a new light!" After that, he would smile and greet me whenever we saw each other. It became much friendlier to face him then.

There was a Taekwondo competition held in Georgia. The Korean Masters were to show a demonstration at the opening ceremony. Everyone was a famous and greatly skilled Master from Atlanta.

Compared to them, I was just a local instructor.

I worked hard as an assistant while the other Masters flew around with the latest kicking techniques. Then it was my turn. I taped two baseball bats together with blue tape and had someone hold it in the air. I was going to do a spin hook kick. The other masters showed their concern for me that two at the same time might be too much. It was rather easy to kick with the bats planted on the ground, but with them held up from one side in the air, it took much more speed and power.

Furthermore, just last week I had broken my heel from kicking a concrete block and bruised the top of my foot from breaking a baseball bat. 'Ah well, I'll just give it my all and rest afterward.' I calmed my breath and spin hook kicked with all the strength that I had. There was a loud "crack!" sound, but only one bat broke. My heel felt like it was burning. I kicked again with a spin hook kick. It didn't break. My heel was so painful that I could put in any strength in it. Suddenly, a hot energy rose from my stomach. I refused to yield. 'In for a penny, in for a pound!' I knew I couldn't use my heels anymore, so I said that I would finish off with a roundhouse kick. But the top of my foot was bruised as well. I did a roundhouse kick as strongly as I could, and the bat just barely broke but had yet to be completely severed. My foot was on fire with pain, and I was about to give up when the audience started cheering in encouragement. I clenched my teeth and kicked a roundhouse one last time. Finally, the second bat completely separated and flew away. Despite my embarrassment from not finishing at once, the audience applauded me for not giving up.

A family among the audience picked up the broken bats and came up to me. They took a photo with me and asked me for my signature on the broken pieces of bats. As I signed, they marveled and asked me if it didn't hurt. How could it not hurt? My foot felt ablaze with fire. I had a hard time all day, trying not to be seen limping.

My Turtle Shell Fist

In a small city called Erie in Pennsylvania, where a lake as big as the sea divides Canada and the United States, our dojang's demo team gave the opening demonstration in a Taekwondo competition. Since the audience itself was comprised of students and Masters that came for the Taekwondo competition, I had to give my all. It was my turn to do fist breaking. I aimed my fist at the 5-inch thick board. Usually, it would not be difficult at all, but the problem was the appearance of the boards. The Grand Master who hosted this competition believed it was meaningless to break a board if it broke too easily. So, to prevent the boards from breaking easily, the competition had square boards instead of rectangular ones. Moreover, the sizes were also larger. I punched out with all my strength. The board smashed with a loud sound that rang around the gym, and the two assistants holding the board fell back onto the ground.

Suddenly my hands felt completely numb as if my fists were not attached to my wrists. I turned around right away and aimed my hand towards the next board to continue with a spear fingertip breaking, but my hands started swelling right in front of my eyes. The pain was excruciating. I felt dread at the pain I knew would come as my fingers hit the board, but I calmed my breath once more and struck my fingers forward.

The board broke again, and I continued with a knife hand breaking, then finished off with a reverse knife hand breaking, before bowing and coming off stage.

I walked out under the pretense that everything was okay, but it was so painful that I didn't know what to do. At the end of the opening ceremony, people came to ask for a handshake, which I couldn't refuse. I smiled and accepted all their hands. They would squeeze my hands heartily, telling me how they were impressed, and even my hair stood up in pain. Enduring the pain each handshake brought, I felted hazy and suffocated to the point where I thought I might collapse. When I finally hid in a corner and looked down at my hand, it looked like a blown-up rubber glove.

After a while, my fist regained its strength and felt much better. I thought it had fully recovered and did another power breaking. My hand broke that day, with a bone sticking out from the back of my hand. It was unbelievably painful.

These days, my severed ligaments, heels, foot, shoulder, fist, wrists, etc., and injuries from head to toe due to my repeated power breaking practices visit every day as chronic pain. I think to myself; this might be what a bone disease feels like. I put my body through too much because I was confident in my health, and this is how I ended up. After that, I can always 'feel' my body, because I am always in pain. It was the harsh result of behaving recklessly and not caring for my body in my youth.

Reviving Traditional Training

Sometimes, I like to go on outdoor training excursions with fellow black belts. In martial arts films, the main characters are always trapped in a temple or a cabin deep in the mountains, isolated from the world and trained rigorously by their Masters. Then when they finally leave, they conquer the nation with their skills.

Sometimes, my students ask if Master Lee has also trained in a mountain or a temple. "Of course!" Eyes turn around with surprise. As a student, my day started with an early morning run, up to the temple in the mountain where I could look down and see my whole town. My morning training routine was to run up and down the stone steps of the temple or run around the temple for physical training. I would drink a bowl of the mountain's mineral water and come down. During summer, I would undergo off-season training in a pleasant and fresh valley and do some intensive physical training. I also remember catching fish and cooking spicy fish stew with it.

Two young black belts in their early twenties, Paul and Nathan, wanted to undergo traditional training like they had seen in the movies. They persistently asked me if I could train them like that, pleading that they would do everything I told them to do. They even wanted to experience the traditional punishments, where the Master would whip his disciple with a stick for his wrongdoings. 'They don't know anything, huh.' So, I told them to write up a vow, in which they would not hold me responsible for any deaths or injuries that may happen during training. That if they wrote it up, I would set up a time to train them. However, the next day, they really came in with a statement, written and signed! "Is that so? All right, I will show you how it works!" I attached a condition that they could drop out anytime if it became too hard, as this was a voluntary battle with themselves. "If you feel like dying, then give up on your own accord!" The young men vowed that they would never give up.

I took them into a deserted mountain early on a weekend morning. I drove along a mountain path for a long time and stopped the truck at a dead-end. From then on, we walked. I had a rucksack full of water bottles, lunch boxes, and all kinds of necessary equipment, including a first aid kit, just in case. And finally, I carried a wooden sword at my side.

The first step was hauling logs. I told each of them to bring logs as big as their body. "Wherever you go today, this log goes with you! Whether you carry it or drag it, you go with it until the end." I first had them tie a rope to the end of the log and pull it up all the way to the top of the mountains. "Let's go!" I followed them wearing my rucksack. As soon as we began, they were soaked in sweat and panting for breath. "Why? Is it hard? You can always drop out." They replied that they would never give up.

When we finally arrived at the top of the mountain, I gave them some time to catch their breath. Then I took out two round metal balls and threw them hard down the mountain slope. They stared at the balls rolling away, undoubtedly wondering what they were supposed to do. "Run down right now to pick up a ball and come back. If you're late, you die. Go!" The two ran down as if they had caught fire. When they came up with their balls, I threw them down again, over and over. They would start to run down to catch the ball but end up rolling themselves down with it instead. After a while, their legs turned to jelly, and they would crawl up the mountain on their hands and knees like turtles. At this point, they couldn't help but feel parched. I opened a water bottle and drank from it myself. Then I slowly poured the remaining water onto the ground. "You run down and back up before I empty this water bottle. You'll only drink the remaining water. Run!" After a brief stare at the water sinking into the earth, they scrambled to run down as fast as they could. They emptied the water bottle, exclaiming that the water felt so sweet after the hardship.

They climbed along the steep mountain slope, all the while kicking, kicking while running through the forest trees, jump-kicking tree branches, jumping while climbing rocks, etc. "Tie your feet with a bicycle tube onto a tree trunk and kick one thousand times! Wind your hands with metal chains and punch the air one thousand times! One person can rest while the other trains. Are you relaxing just because I said you could rest? Hang onto that tree like a cicada while you rest!" Hitting dry and dead trees until they broke. Sparring with trees as opponents. Getting hit with my wooden sword if they lagged behind.

Facing and sparring with each other. The one who took a step backward got a hit on his backside with my wooden sword. "Go forward, only forward!" The young men were beaten and dragged around for half a day. But even while screaming and quivering with exhaustion, they endured everything remarkably and never gave up. I had them carry their logs over their shoulders every time we moved our training location. Their logs became heavier and heavier with time.

Next, I made them break their falls on the dry ground of dirt and pebbles. Who couldn't break a fall on a soft mat? A real break-fall is when you can protect yourself in these kinds of places. "Go!" They moaned in pain after one roll. "Continue rolling! If you don't want to, drop out!" They refused to drop out and continued rolling all the while screaming. I became slightly bored by just watching, and reminiscing about my old days training with this specific exercise in the army, I rolled together with them. Rolling on the hard earth, I felt the pebbles dig deeply into my skin. Frowning, I stood up smoothly and asked the students to take off their shirts. Ugh! Good thing I had them write up that agreement... Their backs were bleeding all over, and even their elbows were scrapped badly with flesh and blood showing.

The next step was running through the mountain trails. I set them a destination point that was approximately 2 miles away and told them to start running ahead. "I'm going to start the truck in exactly 5 minutes. I have no intention of braking, so if I catch up to you, you'll become pancakes. Run if you want to survive!" The young men started running with panicked expressions that screamed, "He's not kidding!" A little later, I rolled down the truck window and started playing loud music, while I followed leisurely along the path.

Far off down the path, I could see them running and panting. Suddenly, Paul seemed to sprain his ankle but continued running even while limping. I slowly drove up behind him and called out, "If it's too hard, you should give up," only to be shocked when he turned back to look at me. Paul was running with foam at his mouth and eyes almost rolled up into his head. Alarmed, I told him to get into the car, but he stubbornly retorted through the foam that he would finish the run. I anxiously followed, worried that the young man might actually end up dead. When he finally arrived at our destination, he collapsed onto the ground. I fed him sips of water and some chocolate. After having rested a little, he recovered enough to grin up at me triumphantly.

Lastly, I had them climb up the mountain on all fours, with their palms and feet on the ground. At this point, people with better stamina would have been exhausted. Even I was drained from following them around all day with a heavy rucksack full of water and training equipment. I walked ahead up the mountain, followed by Nathan, then Paul, both who were crawling behind.

Paul, who was climbing at a slow pace far behind me, suddenly screamed, jumped up, and ran past me. "What is it? What's wrong?" Paul yelled back shortly, "Wasp!" At that, the three of us ran straight up the mountain slope like a bullet and across the mountain peak, never once looking back. Only after a long run did we fall into a heap onto the ground, assured that no wasps were following us.

Paul groaned about how he felt something bump into his hands while climbing, and looked up to see countless wasps, surrounding their hive and all seemingly glaring at him. He had run like crazy with the sole thought of survival. We had indeed experienced the fact that mental strength surpasses the limitations of physical force.

Paul then gasped out, "What would a Master do in this situation?" What on earth! "Idiot, a Master wouldn't touch a wasp hive in the first place!" The look in his eyes said, "Just what I expected!" At that point, I too was dead tired. What an exhausting day it had been! Wrapping up the training, I told them to throw their logs into the river. They looked so refreshed throwing their logs away as if to say good riddance. Dirty and shabby, they loaded themselves onto the back of the truck. When we finally came down to the village, the students exclaimed how the world looked so different. They said it felt as if they had been away for a very long time.

Next class, I asked the two to present what happened and how they felt during training. The boys gushed about the training and took off their shirts to show off the scratches on their backs and the bruises on their bodies. The students listened in awe. Their story wasn't without exaggeration but did somewhat sound like the mountain training of legend. The other students were taken aback that it had been so difficult. I think it seemed even more so with their imaginations adding to the story. After that, we scheduled one-day outdoor training every year during the hot season and cold season. It became our dojang's tradition, but only for the black belt students!

One time, we did our winter outdoor training on a December day. The cold spell had frozen up all the puddles in the last few days. However, I still decided to go ahead with our training as scheduled. The cold left as our bodies heated up from running through the woods. However, the highlight of winter training is to enter the ice-cold water! Of course, it is entirely voluntary. I made a large campfire by the creek shore. I would be the first to take off my shirt and jump into the water, and others would follow one by one. To give a more dramatic effect to the nervous black belt students waiting to enter the water, I dropped a fist-sized rock into the frozen pool. How chilling would it be to see the ice crack and crystal-clear ice water erupt up! However, the rock flew up high and, instead of breaking the ice, only got stuck in it. That was how thick the ice was. Everyone looked at me. 'Ah, it's going to be a terrifying day!'

I boldly jumped into the water. I dove in headfirst. It felt like the whole surface of my skin from head to toe was getting cut. I forced myself to stay underwater for as long as I could, and then pulled my body up and out. "Next volunteer!" The volunteers hesitantly jumped in one by one and ran out shrieking. I stayed in the water until the last volunteer had gotten out of the water. When I finally left the water, my feet and legs were numb and frozen, not moving properly. My face was so stiff that I couldn't even say anything.

Although the one-day outdoor training is hard, it is always regarded as a rewarding special event for all participants, full of stories to tell others. In retrospect, experiences of hardships end up as beautiful memories. Our dojang's most memorable event for the black belts is the outdoor training.

I was ROK!

Among the parents who had gone to the military, many had been stationed as United States Forces Korea (USFK). After telling me that they had served in Korea, they would ask me if I was also ROK. 'Rock?' I didn't understand what they meant at first.

The Korean army is ROKA (Republic of Korea Army), while the Marine Corps is ROKMC (Republic of Korea Marine Corps). Because of this, the Korean military was called ROK for short. Every Armed Forces Day, the military organized Taekwondo demonstrations. Kicking with military boots, bare-handed sparring demonstrations against opponents armed with daggers, breaking tiles with the head, all would shock the USFK. The fierce eyes, the chilling shouts of kihap, and the team demonstrations in sync… They didn't seem like groups of humans then, but fighting machines. Even armed with high-tech equipment, the United States military was afraid of Taekwondo. When I introduced myself as an ex-Korean army member and a Taekwondo military instructor, these parents would testify that there were no questions about my skills as a Master.

I have many recollections from my time as a Taekwondo instructor in the army. One time, a US military lieutenant who visited as an exchange officer was attending our unit's operational evaluation. He declared that given a squad of his army, he could destroy a platoon. Compared to the US, capable of launching an offensive with massive supplies to back it up, he had a low opinion of the South Korean military's tactical capability.

But even so, the U.S. lieutenant seemed to be fascinated by Taekwondo and came by to watch whenever he had time. Then, an incident occurred, which he happened to witness. During a sparring session, I hit my opponent with a spin hook kick. He passed out on the spot, bloody with a broken jawbone, and was sent away immediately by ambulance. The soldier was hospitalized at the Armed Forces Capital Hospital and was unable to leave for more than three months. Later, I crossed path with the U.S. lieutenant who was with an interpreter. He looked at me and exclaimed, "Oh, Taekwondo!" and shook his head. So, I asked the interpreter officer to interpret my words to him. "If you give me a squad, I could destroy a platoon."

My father used to tell me stories about serving as military police during the Vietnam War. When a fight broke out in a bar, the U.S. military police could do nothing to stop it. Even when gunshots rang in the air, the already chaotic fight would not break up. These soldiers heard gunfire shots every day in the battlefield, so they didn't even bat an eyelid. But if someone yelled out "Korean military police are coming!", everyone would run away first, panicking, and yelling, "Taekwondo, Taekwondo!" It was because, if things went wrong, they could get seriously injured during the arrest process. Korean military police officers were selected from among the best Taekwondo instructors. In the United States, having served in the Korean army was something to be incredibly proud of, even more so than in Korea. So, I proudly declare, I was ROK!

There is No Ugly Duckling

Some children run wild in the middle of class, and they are on a different level from children I've seen in Korea. They can't control their strength and can't hold still even for a moment. Some also receive psychological counseling. These children would be led into the dojang by their parents. If I ask them what brought them to my dojang, the parents would reply that a psychiatrist had recommended me. They had been told that children learned to behave better when sent to my dojang. At first, I was anxious. 'Why do all the troublemakers come to me? What will happen to the dojang?' But my confidence gradually grew. The "wild and naughty" kids didn't cause much trouble in Taekwondo classes. On the contrary, they would follow instructions eagerly. Sometimes, I would have to ask their parents, "So, what was the problem?" The parents were happily surprised as well. My students never listen to teachers or parents, yet they follow the Master so well!

I tend to act wilder than the children during class. I shout and add kihap and yell out encouragement so that I can overcome our not being able to communicate well with each other. The children who run wild are strong-willed. In other words, they have too much energy. The children can't control their overflowing power, which is why they jump around acting unruly. When a teacher with a weaker will reprimands and scolds them, it doesn't work very well. As these children age, they become like a bull in a china shop. They go around breaking all kinds of school rules.

But when they are at a dojang, they are told, "Run faster, yell louder, kick harder!" In the dojang, the children are told to do things that they would get scolded for at home and school. They can release excess energy through this type of training, and they love it. Not to mention that their Master is someone who breaks bricks and bats with his bare hands. They hear power and authority in his voice. The look in his eyes is different from any other adults they've met. When the children realize, "Ah, I can't go against the Master," they bend their headstrong ways and begin to follow my lead.

Unlike in school, their whines don't work either in the dojang. If they are caught misbehaving, they are sat down across me after class. It is like counseling. I look into their eyes and ask them, "Who am I?" "The Master." "Where are we?" "The dojang." "Why are you here?" "To learn Taekwondo." "What do you have to do to learn Taekwondo?" "Listen to the Master." The answer is easy. "Yes, you know very well. This isn't school, and I'm not your schoolteacher. And I'm certainly not a babysitter. In this dojang, I'm the head and the law. It's one or the other: either you follow the rules or you get kicked out. I've already kicked out several students because they didn't follow my rules. This is your last chance, or you might be up next. If you do that again, I'm throwing you out of my class. It's your choice. Get kicked out or stay here," I tell them sternly. The student deflates, and realizes once again that I'm not someone they can easily mess with.

Taekwondo classes are fun. They can't be anything but fun, what with being able to run around and shouting kihaps and then getting praised for this behavior! And they know that it's a disgrace to be kicked out of such a place. Schoolteachers can only give empty threats, but they believe the Master will go through with expelling them. Therefore, they promise to be on their best behavior from then on. And I let them continue with the lessons. However, it doesn't always work right away. They are often called in and scolded several more times. And gradually, they learn to follow the rules of the dojang. Even when fooling around, if they catch my eyes from a distance, a short and silent conversation occurs. There is no need for words. 'Are you going to continue?' 'No, I'll be good!' It is almost telepathic. They snap to attention as if they had never fooled around. As they gradually get used to it, their minds learn to abide by the rules. Then they learn to control their bodies and follow the rules, even at school.

I also send questionnaires to schoolteachers and parents before promotion tests to ask about the student's attitude at school and at home. Poor results may lead to being disqualified from taking the test. And their names are placed onto a list of expulsion candidates. It shows students that it is their choice whether to be reprimanded or praised.

War can break out between parents who attempt to discipline their children through punishment and their children who refuse to behave. The children are not actually in the wrong. Their behavior is a result of a distorted hormonal balance, and they can't help it. When I call in their children, some parents tell me the children are misbehaving because their child hasn't taken medication that day. I reply that it is a matter of will and has nothing to do with their pills. The students train in the dojang to judge right from wrong and to follow the rules instead of impulses. As they train, they overcome their hormonal imbalances. I see this training as natural therapy. I often have parents of a student taking sedatives informing me happily that, after learning Taekwondo, the doctor reported that their child could stop taking medication.

As I came to understand these children better, I couldn't dislike them any longer. No matter how unruly some children may be at first, they all start to change for the better when they receive their yellow belts. They become ambitious regarding belts. They want to win their next belt quickly, but they know they have to listen to the Master to do so. They come to realize who has authority. Parents and teachers even threaten the children that they will tell the Master if they continue to misbehave. Then the children beg, "Please don't tell Master Lee!" Even if young, the children are not thoughtless. When encouraged and listened to, kids who always get scolded try their best not to cause trouble because they don't want to disappoint me. Seeing them, I get so touched. Seeing them try hard to change their behavior moves me.

Caleb in a Wheelchair

After a demonstration, I was cleaning up when a child in a wheelchair came up to ask if he could learn Taekwondo, too. He was an 11-year-old boy named Caleb. He became paralyzed from the waist-down in a car accident. His father also pleaded with me to accept him as a student somehow. I had always wanted to teach a student like him. I didn't have any experience teaching a disabled student, and so I couldn't straight away integrate him with other students. So, I decided to instruct him once a week for free. I showed him simple techniques that only required the upper body, like blocking and striking, and had him practice at home as homework. The next class, I checked if he had practiced well and went on to teach him multiple techniques.

Caleb was incredibly spoiled by his parents, who gave him everything he asked for. He wanted to decide what he would learn, demanding, "Teach me this! Teach me that!" There was no way I would humor him. "I only teach good children. It's not that Taekwondo makes children good; I don't teach children who are bad from the beginning. I'm the one teaching Taekwondo. You don't get a choice. Do what you are told to do." With that, he gave up his impatient attitude. Later, he was able to join the general class with the other students.

After months of training, it was time for Caleb to take his first promotion test. Watching him lined up with the other students, everyone was worried. I had him demonstrate poom-sae together with other students. From the ready stance, he turned his wheelchair to the left, blocked and struck, and turned to the other side and blocked and struck again. His poom-sae may have been performed without the kicking, but he finished off with the loudest kihap in the group. His eyes and pursed lips radiated a rare seriousness for his age. Even when testing kicking, he lined up with the other students. When it was his turn, he hit the target with his fists, hands, and elbows to compensate for the lack of kicks, and turned back to line up again.

After the one-step sparring and self-defense, Caleb broke his board with such a staggering amount of strength that his wheelchair wobbled. Everyone stood up to applaud for him. At the end of the promotion test, I tied his new belt and shook his hand. And I could see he wasn't the same boy as the day before. He was a new person, burning with the confidence that he could do anything. His father grabbed my hand, teary-eyed, and thanked me over and over. But in fact, I had gained so much from teaching him as well. I now have the confidence that I can teach students with any level of physical ability.

One day, Caleb asked if he could join our dojang's overnight children's program. I was concerned about his use of the bathroom. His father assured me that he could go to the toilet by himself, so I agreed. But while playing a game, the other children didn't go easy on Caleb at all. I fretted internally. 'Don't they feel sorry? Go a little easy on him.' However, I soon saw that it was a needless concern. Caleb didn't go easy on others either, and he was just as skilled as they were.

Relieved I took my eyes off Caleb for a while. When I looked back, I was appalled: the children had grabbed Caleb out of his wheelchair and were running around, dragging his limp legs. Shocked, I was going to stop them when I noticed that the boy was laughing while being dragged along the ground. The grinning children didn't seem to be bullying him at least. I quietly called one of the boys and asked, "What are you kids doing?" Perhaps afraid that he would get scolded, the boy was quick to answer. "We were running and playing, but he can't run in a wheelchair. So, we're helping Caleb." I felt a lump in my throat. The children had opened their hearts and were treating Caleb as an equal friend.

After learning Taekwondo, Caleb took an interest in and challenged himself in various other sports. He now participates in the Paralympics every year and is an active and proud athlete. Caleb is exceptionally skilled at archery. He exercises far more than the average person. He is busy all year round, as he participates in competitions of various sports. He has won many scholarships and even receives money from town fundraisers to support his necessary expenses. He is living a more healthy and energetic life than general fully abled people. Sometimes he drops by the dojang to say hello, and I see that he is no longer that spoiled little boy, but has grown into a strong and confident young man. He tells me that Taekwondo has helped him so much in his life, but I tell him, "It isn't Taekwondo, but your positive and challenging attitude that has made you a stronger person."

Jesse in a Wheelchair

After hearing about Caleb's success, a mother brought in her son. His name was Jesse. He was ten years old, but he looked like a six-year-old. He was born with his disability. I asked him to step down from the wheelchair to check his condition. His legs and waist were bent in 90 degrees in a sitting position, and without his wheelchair, he had to crawl with his hands to move. Due to low-income family circumstances and no one agreeing to teach him, Jesse had no experience in sport or exercises other than his weekly physical therapy. My heart ached for him. I decided to do good and told them to come once a week for free for private lessons.

Jesse was not only small, but he was also weak for his age. Moreover, he could only stretch out his arms halfway and had difficulty bending his thumbs. Even so, I did not give up on him. I would loudly compliment him: Taekwondo wasn't something just anyone could learn, yet you were doing so well. And each time, he would smile brightly and train harder, shouting out kihaps with his tiny voice. Seeing both the child and his mother so happy made it very rewarding.

I was told that he was timid and rarely talked to others, but he would often ask me questions and answer my questions well. One day, I asked him as I always asked other kids, "What do you want to be when you grow up?" His smile immediately dropped, and his face fell. With tears in his eyes, he did not answer. 'Ah! What a mistake!' Despite being young, Jesse had been despairing over his uncertain future. My heart ached for him. I sincerely hoped that Taekwondo would help this child, even if only slightly.

According to his mother, he used not to do anything after school (which was a school for children with disabilities), yet during his training days, he would enthusiastically practice blocking and punching at home and eagerly wait all week for Taekwondo classes. Even I could see his eyes come alive in class.

After a few months, Jesse's posture slowly began to improve. Of course, it was difficult to display the proper moves due to limitations of his body, but he was putting in his all. Is that not what Taekwondo training is truly for? Every time students receive a higher belt through their promotion test, their behavior improves, and they develop self-confidence and pride. This child absolutely needed the self-respect earned through the tests.

However, the situation was more difficult than Caleb's case. Jesse's arm strength was so weak that he even had difficulty changing the direction of his wheelchair by himself. However, I made no exceptions. The harder it was for him to achieve something, the higher his sense of accomplishment would be. He managed to finish his poom-sae, struggling all the while to change the direction of his wheelchair. The people watching with bated breath seemed to be even more nervous for him. A storm of applause broke out once his poom-sae was over. I deliberately paired up with him when testing for the one-step sparring and self-defense. It was a show of consideration on my part, in case the kids thoughtlessly went all out on him. The final test was board-breaking. I chose the thinnest board for him to break with his bare hands, but still the board didn't break on the first attempt. He struck it seven, eight times more with his arm that wouldn't even straighten properly. Yet the board would not break. The disappointment was evident on his face as he started tearing up. The humiliation from sitting in a wheelchair, unable to break what other students broke on their first try, while watched by many people, worked against him as a bigger obstacle. The students and the audience were all overwhelmed, feeling sorry for him. They even seemed to feel reproachful towards me. 'Why isn't Master Lee stopping this? Doesn't he feel sorry?' Jesse looked like he was on the verge of tears.

I stopped what he was doing and asked, "Do you want to get your yellow belt?" "Yes, sir," he replied with a small voice. "Then there is only one way. Break the board. I don't ask people to do things they can't do. I'm asking you because you can do it. Answer me, can you do it?" He answered hesitantly, "Yes, sir…." I yelled, "Your voice is too small! Can you do it?" His voice grew louder with surprise. "Yes, sir!" When their voices become louder, nine out of ten times they succeed. That is because self-confidence is our true inner strength. "Break!" He gritted his teeth, and his eyes flashed with determination. The board broke as his hand struck down. The people around us all stood up, shouted, and applauded. He sheepishly smiled as if to say, "It was nothing." Behind the smiling Jesse, I could see his mother crying wordlessly.

Afterward, I had my black belt students take turns in teaching Jesse. They could make friends with each other, and the seniors learned to use Taekwondo for good things.

I signed up an unknowing Jesse in the annual Kid Talent Search. I told him to compete amid other talented children proudly. He immediately drew attention as he was lifted up the stage stairs in his wheelchair. He then demonstrated self-defense, board-breaking and even nun-chuck demonstrations with his bent arms. It was by far the most popular act and received a standing ovation. A local newspaper took a photo of this as "the best scene of the day," and Jesse became a star in the town due to people recognizing him. There is no need to add how proud his mother was.

As an instructor, there is no greater joy than seeing children grow confident through taekwondo. Taekwondo is a good friend that changed not only my life but also the lives of others who have met me. I always say, "I don't sell Taekwondo in the dojang; I sell confidence."

Why Taekwondo?

Taekwondo is a martial art that uses the leg as its principal means of attack. For Americans, whose lower bodies have weakened from constant sitting, it is the ideal training system to strengthen the lower body and find balance.

It is refreshing to kick a target and shout kihap at the top of your lungs. The pleasure of controlling your breath and focus, then breaking boards does much to relieve stress. In a shoe culture where you wear shoes from when you get out of bed until you get back in, running barefoot is a relief.

Furthermore, kicking techniques always use the spine and pelvis, the center of the body, and make them more flexible, strong, and robust. In fact, once you practice kicking the target, your body feels refreshed in a way that you cannot experience with any other exercises. Moving the hip joint is, in particular, much more significant than any other activity. That is because the pelvis becomes relaxed from stretching. Therefore, even those who have exercised in a fitness center are impressed by the refreshing taste of sweating, shouting kihap, and kicking targets all together.

The student of Taekwondo also overcomes a mind complacent because of a self-indulgent lifestyle and a solitary, self-centered life through disciplined training with a group of like-minded people. The student develops a desire for a more modest lifestyle. The black belt received at the end of years of hard training and the self-confidence to overcome self-imposed limitations are the most significant gifts of learning Taekwondo.

By causing you to control your breathing and refreshing your mind, Taekwondo training is a short break from a hectic daily life. It is a moving meditation practice that re-energizes the body and mind. Once you finish your training, you are recharged, ready to go back to your life. It is because of this that Taekwondo training is my vocation.

Mr. Bill and the Adult Training

The adult population that learns Taekwondo is gradually decreasing. The reason is simple. It is because Taekwondo is hard for adults. People are still young in mind, but they feel weak in the legs and out of breath during Taekwondo training. Even people who were very fit in their youth find it difficult to train at the dojang. They constantly compare themselves with the teenagers running next to them. They see their bodies breaking down from age and despair. In the end, they give up and decide to play something like golf.

Mr. Bill, with his white hair, was a lawyer. When I asked him something, he would give me a straightforward and articulate answer. He was a highly educated person. But in Taekwondo classes, I couldn't help feeling sorry for him. He must have been one of the most untalented people in Taekwondo that I had ever seen. Even after four years of training, he was unable to memorize the poom-sae. He was so stiff that his kicks and movements were awkward. Unfortunately, his body coordination, balance, and flexibility had barely improved over the years. Yet it was obvious that he had enjoyed Taekwondo training even with his limitations. When performing a kicking sequence with more than three steps, he would forget each next step. He stayed a red belt even while his junior students all became black belts. Despite this, he continued to work hard.

A week before his black belt promotion test—finally, after four years—

Mr. Bill lost his confidence. He had always smiled brightly, never showing his troubles outwardly, but he was in despair right before the promotion test. He told me that he was sorry, but that he couldn't do it anymore. He was serious. He had been working so hard with perseverance until now, and if he gave up at this point, he would never pick it up again. I sat down next to him to help him regain his confidence.

Ki, life energy, flows inside our body. The flow of energy in the body starts from the feet and moves up to the top of the head. This flow can summarize the human life. A baby's energy resides in his/her feet. So even when lying down, a baby will keep wriggling his/her feet and kicking his/her blanket. Later on, babies try to stand up with their feet even without being taught. It is because the energy is directed to the legs. There is no need for other games during infancy. Just running is fun enough. Children want to run around everywhere because they need to release the energy filling up their legs.

In adolescence and adulthood, the energy rises higher and becomes concentrated in the lower belly. You become interested in the other sex. Vigorous reproductive energy becomes abundant. During middle age, the energy rises to the heart. You wish to spend your life on something you truly love. When you finally reach old age, the energy floats up to the head. The body is out of energy, and everything physical becomes hard. The head is restless, full of all kinds of memories and delusions. Your sleeping time reduces, and your thoughts are always moving. In the end, when the energy escapes through the crown of the head, the body is discarded. Without energy, the body dies.

If we equate this human journey with breathing, the distance a breath travels from the lower abdomen to the nose is a lifetime. A baby naturally breathes with abdominal respiration. His/her breath is soft and deep. He/she may be delicate and weak, but his/her dynamic vitality grows miraculously every day. But in time, the breath slowly rises and turns into thoracic respiration. We adults rely on our lungs and breathe by expanding our chest. Our breath is not deep. That is why adults easily run out of breath, while children can run all they want. Once we get older or become physically weak, our breathing climbs up to our shoulders, so our shoulders shake when we breathe. With increasing age, our breathing fills our jaws. It is a sign of imminent death. When our gasping breath reaches our noses, we reach the end of life.

I told Mr. Bill to think about where he was in life. He was probably somewhere around late middle age. The energy gathers towards his upper body and his legs naturally become weak. While his breath rises and grows faster, his body becomes stiffer. It is the law of nature. Being unable to kick like young adults wasn't something he should be worried about. I explained to him that if he kept on slowly and steadily, the energy would go back down to his legs and he would be able to improve his movements and live a healthier life.

The health of the body comes from the spine. If the spine—the pillar that supports the body—collapses, the whole-body collapses. To keep this spine upright and healthy for a long time, training the lower body is essential. A tree with a weak root cannot stand. In other words, I explained, kicking and poom-sae help to preserve the spine and redirect energy towards the lower body; the goals of training are not solely breaking boards and memorizing movements.

His breathing was also short. That was because his breath floated in his chest. When a person loses his or her breath, even the strongest one will break. Therefore, we can lead healthy, energetic and young lives only if we drag down our breathing to our lower abdomens and take breaths deeply and slowly. I advised him that he should follow movements to the point that his breath does not reach his jaw, that when he starts losing breath, he should control his breathing first and then start again.

The purpose of adults' Taekwondo training is to live younger by returning energy to their weak legs and keeping their rising breath down. That was the goal of Taekwondo training that Mr. Bill needed to concentrate on, not just to run and break boards like teenagers. Mr. Bill's greatest personal strength was that he had continued to train regularly according to his own pace without giving up. He still had a week left. I made him stand, encouraging him to try one more time together with me. Mr. Bill thanked me as he stood up. And he passed the promotion test with flying colors and became a proud black belt. Mr. Bill, a slow student regarding techniques but an honor student with his efforts, progressed further skill-wise once he received his black belt.

Adults quickly understand their limitations through this explanation of the life cycle of ki. Taekwondo is a martial art for people to train and develop themselves. True self-defense is to protect oneself from rusting with time. We must impress upon people that adults are the ones that need Taekwondo training the most. Our dojang often has students sit in meditation 5 minutes before class ends. It is to control their excited minds and breathing. We put on traditional Korean music and relax with our legs half-crossed to calm our harsh breathing, close our eyes, and sit in meditation to ease our minds. Adults love this time. They feel a short but profound sense of peace. I have found that even children quite enjoy this time. To protect our bodies, we must first protect our minds.

Examples of Perseverance, Justin and Jared

As an instructor, you will meet many students with different characteristics. Some of them show great talent for Taekwondo from the moment they wear their white belts. They are quick to learn and bypass me just after a few attempts. It is a wonder why these people do anything else besides Taekwondo! On the other hand, some people have hardly any talent in Taekwondo. It's difficult to teach them anything. They are unable to follow well, and they do not understand no matter how many times I explain and demonstrate. They progress much more slowly than their fellow students and eventually fall behind in belt promotion. They make me anxious as their instructor.

But after one year, two years, three years, I am always surprised to see those who remain to receive their black belts. The talented students are usually physically fit and have sharp eyes for learning things. They are good at various things other than Taekwondo and many times leave Taekwondo training for other pursuits. It is often the less talented students that remain and become black belts. They know nothing but Taekwondo, and they don't really get noticed in other sports. I cannot help but sigh, wondering how I am left with Taekwondo idiots. However, on second thought, I remember that person who didn't have sharp eyes or talent, who was a slow learner and was unwelcome, who was clearly lacking... Me! And yet, 40 years later, here I am, a Taekwondo Master.

Students who can be even slower than people with physical disabilities are those with intellectual disabilities. I put these students in the same regular training session as others and help them progress. I have had autistic students who could not speak or understand what was being said. Because people rarely want to partner with these students, I have them follow practice alone and pair up with them myself when they need an opponent.

Twelve-year-old Justin was my first student with an intellectual disability. He always watched his younger sister train, and I accepted him as my student because of his father's earnest requests. Living with a working single father, Justin's uniform was often unclean, and he would have food smeared on his face, in his messy hair, on his clothes. My wife would take him aside whenever she saw him, to clean him up with a wet towel.

In the beginning, he would stand halfway turned toward the wall and look at me with unfocused eyes from the back of the classroom. There was no way he could progress like that. I had to hold and move his hands and feet. Even then, he would barely manage to do a few movements. At first, I was uncomfortable and tired because of how much I had to attend to him. Little by little, however, I started to feel at ease about his presence. He began to follow class a little. He would frequently stop following and stand to do nothing, but he wasn't interrupting or making others uncomfortable. And when I walked to him to hold his hands and feet, he would smile happily at me.

One day, I was teaching a series of one-step sparring moves. The movements divided into six steps that included blocking, kicking, twisting, punching, and flipping over. It was something we had learned last class, but none of the students were able to follow correctly. That moment, my eyes caught Justin moving alone clumsily in the back. 'Could it be?' It looked to me as if Justin was remembering and copying all the moves. I called Justin forward. "Justin, you try it!" Everyone seemed to be thinking, 'what can he do?' When I punched my fist towards him, he avoided it, then blocked, kicked, twisted back, hit, tripped me with his leg, and punched again. His movements were sloppy but correct. And then he turned towards the wall and grinned to himself. Boom! Everyone looked like they had been hit on the head with a hammer. So, did I. After that, I asked Justin to demonstrate other moves. Slowly but surely, Justin copied every step precisely. Children who pride themselves on their intelligence tend to watch me cavalierly and follow however they want. But Justin, who we thought was standing and staring at the wall, had always been looking sideways at me!

After that, no one could ignore Justin. When I paired Justin up with a partner, he would copy his partner's movements. When standing in line to kick targets, he would chase the person in front of him and copy the kicking sequences clumsily but very well.

Just like that, Justin began to melt into the class. Even if he couldn't memorize everything, he would copy the person next to him to practice his poom-sae and breaking. He passed his promotion tests one by one.

He didn't disturb the class at all, to the point that on some days, I could not even remember if Justin had come to class or not. Days that I would ask, "Was Justin here today?" increased. He blended in with the other students that well.

When he came to the dojang led by his mother, Jared was already a 19-year-old young man with a beard. He was much bigger than I was. Because of his intellectual disability, he could not have a driver's license issued, and his mother had to take him everywhere. Due to his autism, he never spoke with others and never even met eyes with them. He also had never played any sports. When I asked him to do push-ups, he trembled in position and collapsed down a few seconds later. He couldn't keep his balance either. Despite his big size, his hands were weak and frail like balloons. His body's rigidity and physical strength were no better than an old man in his 80s.

In any case, he attended a white belt class full of little kids. Of course, I didn't really expect him to yell kihap either. A few kicks and punches later, he would go pale and breathless. It was too dangerous to ask him to practice breaking his fall, as he couldn't control his limbs adequately. Thus, I ended up being his partner most of the time. I worried that he might get injured from practicing alone.

But there was one way in which Jared was excelled above others, and he received an award for it—the Attendance Award. He didn't have any choice but to follow his parents and grandparents to class, as he couldn't drive anyway, but there was hardly ever a day that he missed class all year around. Despite my initial belief that he probably wouldn't last long since he wasn't learning much, this is his 8th year of attending the dojang.

At first, he didn't understand anything and made no progress. Considering his age and size, I couldn't keep him in the lower belt classes with the young children forever. Thus, I still had him to go through the promotion test once every several months, even if it required more work on my part. I gave him private lessons and extra instruction, and truthfully, it was hard. When it came to the point that I couldn't wait for him to get ready any longer, I gave him belts even if he just copied the person next to him. Like that, I stubbornly dragged him up to red belt.

Finally, the black belt promotion test! In our dojang, you can only go through the promotion test if you have learned and know how to use various techniques. Therefore, Jared continued to have his name up for the test, only to be canceled, several times. Sometimes, I would scold Jared out of frustration, even knowing his circumstances. But Jared never frowned or expressed anger. The only words he would say were, "Yes, sir!" And I would feel sorry and ashamed for scolding him.

Jared passed his black belt promotion test four and a half years later, and he became a 1st-degree black belt. He has since become so strong that it is painful to receive his hits even protected by two heavy practice body targets. I always have to remind him to go easy on his opponents so that they don't get hurt. His kihap is so loud that I tell my other black belts to "shout out your kihap like Jared." I show the black belt students one-step sparring or self-defense movements that are slightly complex. I often demonstrate just once and tell them to practice by themselves, because I assume that they can just do it since they are black belts. More often than not, the students become lost. When that happens, I call out Jared. He follows my lead and readily demonstrates complicated moves. Then the rest of the black belts can't help but be humbled.

More recently, Jared learned a series of 40-step long staff-sparring with a partner. One wrong move would get you beaten by your opponent's rod. Everyone was busy trying to memorize all the movements. Some were having difficulty learning everything even after a month. But Jared remembered all the moves. The smart guys would make excuses, saying that there are too many moves or that they are too complicated. Then I would retort, "What's so complicated? You just aren't paying attention!" and call out Jared to have him spar with me. After that, no one would have anything to say. Jared never loses focus during class. He only watches at me, whatever I do. That is why he is one of my best students. I have never asked any other students to treat Jared with special consideration. Nor have I ever treated Jared differently. I only want him to live ordinarily with others.

Now, Jared goes out of his way to say "hello" and talk to others first. Despite his autism, he participates in conversations in the dojang. He spends a lot of his time alone, mostly reading hard and tedious history books. Sometimes, after class, he tells my wife or me about everything from the Cold War to modern North and South Korea's politics. Other students' jaws drop at that. Of course, the problem is that this isn't necessarily the place for these subjects, but students are still impressed, 'Wow, he can hold that kind of conversations with the Master?' If he goes on for too long, I sometimes cut him off in case it's too much for the other students. "Jared, let's stop with politics and history today." I ask my wife, "Could Jared maybe be a genius?" There are times when I think he might be an autistic genius, like in the classic movie Rain man, starring Dustin Hoffman.

Jared works at Walmart at night. His job is to stock shelves with new items during the night. He leaves the dojang soaked in sweat every time, so he gets home to take a shower and then goes to work right away. Of course, his family still drives him around. The U.S. is full of unemployed young people. Even those who are perfectly healthy barely get by because they cannot or do not get a job. Yet Jared is a proud worker who has a job and earns his keep. Furthermore, he is a black belt, which is a difficult achievement even for non-disabled people. Jared is now a 2nd degree black belt. He passed a public promotion test, in front of 10 judges, his whole family and hundreds of other people in audience. The 27-year-old Jared has become the best role model of civility and perseverance, of hard work and accomplishment.

The Dojang Swept Away by a Flood and Visiting Angels

One particularly rainy summer in 2010, I got a call on an early Monday morning. I received news that the dojang got flooded. "Flooded?" At that time, I didn't quite catch the meaning of the word. There was a small stream behind the dojang, but it wasn't anything that could cause flooding. I wasn't too worried until I turned on the TV. It was showing a flood zone that looked eerily familiar. "No, don't tell me!" The large parking lot in front of my dojang where I always parked my car was full of people on boats. A massive dam built on the upper region of the small stream had broken due to the heaviest local downpour in 100 years. When I finally got to the dojang, I saw that it had become a swimming pool.

When the water finally drained out, the dojang was utterly desolate. The floor mats and the walls were covered with mud, and the training equipment was all drenched and useless. I stood there, staring blankly at my dojang. I didn't know where to begin. I had spent years nailing and hammering the place into a decent school, but now everything was gone. Behind me, one by one, my students and their families gathered together. They said they had come to help me with repairs. They asked me what do to, but I had never experienced a flood before and had no idea. One of the students suggested that the mats may be usable again if we washed and disinfected them. Deciding that I should at least try to save the floor mats, I took them outside. The carpet underneath smelled rotten. I tore out the whole carpet that had been under the 300 mat puzzle pieces. It was hard to pull off as the carpet had been glued to the ground for decades. After barely managing to remove the carpet, I sat on my knees and cut away the remaining glue with a knife. Then I washed the mat, the floor, and the wall several times with water, sprayed disinfectant, and then wiped each of them with a sponge. For the next few days, I dried the mat outside and vacuumed the water from the floor and walls. Then I turned on a large electric fan and dried up the room again. Throughout this tedious process, my students voluntarily came to assist me. Several adult students even took 3 or 4 days off work to help me. They brought all the necessary tools from their home and bought whatever was lacking with their own money. I had done nothing but teach them Taekwondo and get paid for it, yet these people thought of me as family. Realizing that, I burst into tears. Every evening, I took their hands and thanked them again and again, but this was not enough to express the magnitude of my gratitude.

Thinking that I couldn't be seen being discouraged or lazy to those who came to my aid, I worked even harder. I tried to carry every heavy thing I could and more. Other than that, all I could do was to buy the students pizzas and drinks. Although it wasn't even a proper meal, the students thanked me and ate. Seeing these people taking on such rough work, I felt like they were wingless angels sent to me by heaven.

The dojang was repaired in a week thanks to the students, and I could start classes again. However, although I had disinfected and dried everything, mold had already begun to bloom on the damp walls. It became difficult to breathe from the musty smell. I was forced to search for a new location to move into and decided to relocate to an old building about a mile away. It was too old to be used as a dojang in its current state. But I had no choice. I decided to move over in the month before the weather became cold.

To reduce building reparation and labor costs, I went out early in the morning. Hammering, sawing, nailing painting, etc., I did it all. Then I would go to school and teach Taekwondo. When class ended, I went back to the building and repaired it until dawn. At first, the students seemed doubtful, seeing the place looking like an abandoned warehouse. But exactly a month later, when I finished painting in and out, it became a decent place. Of course, it was only half the size of the flooded dojang, but it had its charm. The students were also surprised, seeing the crumbling warehouse turn into a bright and cozy place within a month. "Master Lee, did you do this all by yourself? How do you know how to do these things?" It is not because I have any talent. I have merely gained from experience the belief that any problem can be gradually solved as long as I keep trying. I did so much carpentry work each time I opened a dojang, that it was getting hard to tell whether I was an instructor or a building manager! Regardless, I felt proud that I didn't just sit down helplessly hoping for help to come my way.

From time to time, I have encountered hardships that tried to trip me on my path. And each time, I learned that the power to overcome such difficulties did not come from money, but from the people around me that support me like family.

My dojang's family helped and supported me when I was numb from the flood. I am forever in their debt. They have shown me love through sharing their time for my sake, and I wish to repay their love through Taekwondo.

Talent Show

Three students known for their weak presence in the dojang came up to me. "We're going out in the school talent show the day after tomorrow. Please help us." "What? You are?"

Kennedy, who was thin enough to appear like a famine victim, Justin, who was just lanky, and Destiny, who had a bigger build than even I. These three students were fifth graders, all of the same age.

"Why are you telling me this now? Did you pass the audition?" The school had given them a free pass, hearing that Master Lee would be coaching them. It was the school showing consideration for me, as they knew me well. Inevitably, I squeezed my brains all night out for a plan. However, when I instructed them the next day, I realized it would not work.

A Taekwondo demonstration should be something that is "quick and accurate, break with a single strike!" but the adjectives that described this team were "awkward, sloppy, confusing." In addition, they failed to memorize the order of the short demonstration, bumping into each other, tripping down and making a fuss as if they were carrying out home appliances from a house on fire.

"It can't be helped. Change of plans! We're going to change concepts! From now on, your concept is comic action! Run and kick, fly and fall flat!" After the short training session, I sent them home, telling them to please, just follow the training.

The next day, the children arrived at the dojang even before class with flushed faces. I was worried what jeremiads they may have done. "Did you do everything we practiced without forgetting?" And the answer was unexpected. "Master Lee, we won first place!" "What?"

To tell the truth, a talent show coexists with an uncomfortable truth. It is a place divided between 'the stage of talented children,' where good-looking and smart children with thick make-up dance and sing and play instruments and 'the untalented children' who merely applaud from the sides. Yet in this garden of 'talented' friends, these 'untalented' children boldly sent out a challenge.

I watched a video clip they had filmed. The children played out comic actions in tune with the comical background music and yelled out unusually relentless kihaps. It could not be funnier if it was on purpose. Children's laughter, exclamations, and applauses continued endlessly. These boys who just floated around invisibly in the classroom were showing off their Taekwondo skills. Everyone went crazy with giggles and laughter. Furthermore, unlike during practice, they did their individual board-breaking parts well. Unlike usual, they bellowed out kihaps that overwhelmed the audience, turning cartwheels with their hands on the ground and breaking the boards.

Finally, Kennedy stepped onto Justin's back and jumped up, kicking the board that was so high up it seemed impossible to reach with his short legs, and landed. Of course, it was a success after four previous mistakes, but their friends applauded even louder at their determination not to give up until the end.

After the show, their classmates crowded around them, saying 'I won't ever mess with you in the future!" "Doesn't your hand hurt?" "Can you sign this broken board?" They told me that the first time in school, they were at the center of the conversation. These children were so endearing that I embraced them tightly.

The show ended in merely 4 minutes and 30 seconds, but through this, the children confidently broke a barrier in life, namely bullying. And these children have made me realize that doing your best at something can be more beautiful than doing impressively well at something. As they ended their final times in elementary school in 5th grade, when these children return to school as middle school students, I am positive that they will no longer be bullied but welcomed as a proud member of their peer groups.

The Word that Gives Strength

Peyton, a five-year-old girl, who seemed to be in a good mood after a fun class, came over to hug me. She said, "Master Lee! Today is the best day of my life! You are the best master I have ever had!" and then hopped away. I laughed for a long time at her elderly way of speaking. At any rate, my tired body felt energized at those words. I always want to have words to say to my students that can give strength, as this child did, and I always regret not being able to.

Living as a Master, one meets many people. Sometimes we laugh together and sometimes we cry together. Therefore, the role of a Master does not just end with merely transferring techniques. In many cases, we also take upon the role of a counselor.

Counseling children who get bullied or who hate studying are in fact relatively easy. From those who lost their jobs and are facing financial difficulties, those who lost their desire to live from serious depression, to those whose family member is terminally ill, each of these problems are difficult to give a straightforward answer.

All I can do is listen to their frustrated stories and say a few words to comfort them. I can only hope that the words out of my mouth become a comfort, becomes a support and becomes even the slightest help to my trainees.

Yet even just with that, people seem to feel a weight off their mind. They become a little more peaceful, and then at some point thank me, saying that their problem had been resolved. Even though I had not actually done anything for them. Like this, when I exchange words from deep inside with my students, I feel both my mind and theirs growing ripe.

The kind word has the power to penetrate through the body and pierce through the clogged energy deep within the mind. So, a comforting word that gives hope can even save someone who wishes for death. Therefore, I believe that every word a Master speaks must always try to be good words.

The Spider Web

There was a palm-sized spider web on the corner floor of the dojang I had just moved into. Like a house grudgingly built by an unskilled carpenter, the spiderweb was nothing but a few entangled strings. There was no sign of the whereabouts of the lazy carpenter. "How will you survive if you're that lazy?" I kibitzed and brushed aside the spider web with a foot. The next day, however, there was an identical web on the same spot. "That's the one from yesterday." I brushed it away with my foot again without giving it any thought. But the next day, the same-shaped spider web hung again on the same spot. "Hey, he's stubborn." I wondered if I was being a little heartless, as I was in the same circumstance of having to rent in another's house. Nevertheless, every day I kicked away that spiderweb that was the size of a handspan.

However, no matter how many times I demolished it, the unlicensed structure would be rebuilt the next day. "Huh, look at that, would you?" At some point, out of stubbornness, I started the day by kicking away that spiderweb upon arriving at the dojang. The repeated monotony of everyday life soon becomes forgotten. The days went placidly by. I would remove the web and the spider would weave another.

Then one day, I was startled into my senses. "It's already been three years!" For the past three years, I had been kicking away spider webs and the spider had been weaving them over again. Can a tiny spider live that long? It cannot be. The web was there before I moved in, so I guess the grandfather spider gave birth to a son, and the son gave birth to a grandson, and the work of weaving a spider web at that spot had been passed on through the family.

Once upon a time, a general, defeated in a battle and chased, hid in a small tunnel. At the entrance of the narrow tunnel, a spider was weaving a web. Mourning his poor situation, he unconsciously scattered the web with his hand, so the spider began to spin a web again. When the spider finished webbing, he unconsciously broke the web once again. Yet, the spider did not give up and spun a new web.

'Now even an insignificant creature is looking down on me!' The general broke the spider web for the seventh time out of spite, but the spider silently weaved its eighth web.

'How stubborn! It should have given up by now!' That moment as he blamed the spider's stupidity, the enemy's search troops suddenly approached the tunnel. The general lay flat face down and held his breath, thinking this would be the moment of his death. However, a veteran enemy soldier turned back with his colleagues, saying that looking at the spider web blocking the entrance, no one would have gone inside.

A spider web in its natural state does not break easily even in heavy rain and wind. So even now in the military, when chasing an enemy, soldiers are trained to chase after broken spider webs and quickly skip places where the spider webs are intact.

The general, saved by the indomitable spirit of a persistent spider, gained great enlightenment and is said to have gained his feet, making a great contribution to the country. The idiom 'indomitable spirit', that refers to achieving something through endless endeavors in spite of many failures, derives from this spider's web.

When you open your mind, there is a great deal to learn even from insignificant creatures. They show such sincerity in carrying out the work that heaven has entrusted to circulate Nature. This is a lesson that humans must see and learn.

Vocational Consciousness

My middle school nephew came to the United States for school break. During the month that he stayed, I gave him daily assignments that would help him learn some English. I had him doing Taekwondo with American friends in my dojang and conversing with someone of the same age for an hour every day. I then tested if he had done it right. I had him repeat aloud what he had learned that day in a horse-riding stance and didn't let him up until he recited everything. His legs would fall asleep while he stammered words out. If he tried to finish and stand up half-heartedly, I would push him back down. "Our family motto is to earn your keep. If you can't earn your keep, you'll keep doing the horse-riding stance." I tested him like that for 5-10 minutes, but it appeared that these tests were painful for my nephew.

There was a meeting I had to attend in Atlanta, so I took my nephew with me to give him a tour of the place. One of the Grand Masters asked him, "Are you having fun in America?" My nephew's expression said it all. He'd come expecting to play and have fun, but his uncle was making him do horse-riding stances every day. Hearing that, the Grand Master replied, "Well, horse-riding stance for 5 minutes isn't that much. I have been doing horse-riding stances for 50 years now." Everyone laughed out loud at that, except for my nephew who was pale with horror. He may have resolved then never to do Taekwondo. Horse-riding stance for 50 years! Although his words were half in jest, I couldn't help but feel respect. He was a professional who had walked a path of one way of life. There are many Grand Masters who still wear their uniforms to teach their students every day, even after reaching their seventies. That would be impossible without a real vocational consciousness.

It would be a marvelous thing to know one's vocation. Someone who believes his or her path is a mission from heaven and regards it as his or her vocation—is not that a professional? It makes me think. Do I have this sense of vocation and professionalism?

If we believe that this is our path, it is time to continue to strengthen our sense of vocation again and again. Just as one cannot imagine a soulless expert, only a person who puts his or her heart and soul into his or her path can become a real professional. If you are a proper self-disciplining professional, the heavens will surely know and help you on your way.

Chapter 4. True Form of Self Defense

Mr. Smith

Mr. Smith is a respectable gentleman who never talks negatively. One day, Mr. Smith came into the dojang with a limp. He said he was taken in by the police in handcuffs and had spent the night in lockup. This is his story. His neighbor was a rude man, a soldier who had been discharged. The previous day, he kicked the door and barged into Mr. Smith's home while yelling and causing a scene. At the time, the only people home were Mr. Smith's wife and daughter.

Alarmed, his wife hurriedly called Mr. Smith. When he quickly left work to get back home, he found that the neighbor was angered because the Smith's dog had pooped in his yard. There was no fence in between, but after checking, it was clearly on Mr. Smith's own yard. Mr. Smith civilly told the man that there was no longer any need to make a scene as this was his yard. He turned back when a fist suddenly came from behind. He could see spots and his glasses were thrown off. Suddenly, the two were dogpiled on top of each other, fighting. The police arrived and arrested both men for assault.

Mr. Smith was released from the jail cell—somewhere he had never in his life imagined he would be—after paying his expensive bail. In the next several months, after many lengthy court debates, he received a verdict of guilty for mutual combat. The incident concluded with payment of a substantial fine.

I could not understand. 'What? The man kicked door and yelled to a house with only women inside, made a scene and used violence first. Mr. Smith was locked in a cell and paid fines because he defended himself? Should he have been beaten helplessly in front of his wife and daughter until the police arrived? Isn't this the same country that found a man not guilty when he shot and killed his neighbor who tried to enter his yard while fighting about garbage disposal problems? They said it was an act of self-defense against home invasion. But it's an assault when you punch back someone who trespassed and attacked?' I had a hard time establishing what the extent of self-defense was in the United States.

Mr. Smith also grumbled about the harsh law. I asked if he at least won the fight, to which Mr. Smith suddenly grinned and replied as if he had been waiting for the question. While taking photos at the police station, he had implored, "I've never gotten into a fight in my entire life! I would be crazy to pick a fight with someone who used to be a professional soldier. Look at the bruises on my face." To that, the police retorted, "That's nothing! The other guy's face is a total mess!" He couldn't remember everything clearly, but he did apparently win. Mr. Smith thanked me, saying that he had been able to build up his body for the past few months through Taekwondo. I was satisfied, too! I would have been greatly upset if the kind Mr. Smith had only received the beating.

After each promotion test, I sit students down and ask them questions.

Each time, I ask, "Why do you learn Taekwondo?" One of the answers that usually comes out is that it's for self-defense. Then I ask again. "Does anyone hit you? Have you ever been attacked? Why do you need self-defense?"

"Most of you will never have to get into fistfights. Unless your life is at actual risk, using Taekwondo for self-defense will even have you paying a greater legal price. Therefore, Taekwondo is only the last card to choose in that situation." They seem to want to ask why they should learn Taekwondo if that is the case. "Besides, I am paid to teach you Taekwondo, but you don't really take anything from me!" Come to think of it, they realize that this seems to be true. All I do is shout and they are the ones doing the hard training. It's bewildering. However, I tell them that I sell self-confidence. Learning self-defense with punching and kicking is just a bonus from Taekwondo training. Self-confidence is the most necessary form of self-defense in American society.

Criminal psychologists have investigated the prisoners in prison. Whom do they choose as their target? On first thought, you would think that they go without second thought for a small and weak person, but it is not so. They choose someone who looks the most insecure on the streets; that is the easiest target. Someone who walks with shoulders and eyes down, who looks afraid, who does not seem sensitive to the surroundings. On the other hand, someone who straightens his or her shoulders, opens his or her eyes wide, regardless of gender or size? Criminals avoid people who talk energetically and walk vigorously because they sense that they will not be easy to deal with. Criminals are cowardly people. Why would they deliberately choose challenging targets when they could go for the easy ones?

The most frequent crisis that young American students face is bullying and school violence. Who becomes an outcast and who becomes a victim of bullying? The same is true for adults. They are often the ones with unsure and timid eyes, behavior, and way of speaking.

That is why I always emphasize, "Never look like easy prey!" I tell my students to have a confident look, a bright and friendly way of speaking, and a vigorous gait and always to stand tall. At the same time, I teach them that gentle and kind body language and genuine friendships are the real art of self-defense. If you become a kind and considerate person, good friends will naturally gather around and protect you.

The United States is a country where many students are not free from drugs. In many cases, a problem student is bound to be involved in drugs. Usually, people learn to use drugs by hanging out with the wrong friends. Drugs are not something you can solve with self-defense. Therefore, building your space, your own world to hang out with good friends is the real self-defense in such dangerous situations.

The same goes for adults. At work, people need to have a confident posture in their respective positions. Life is always a series of problems. If you face your issues confidently, you will have a higher chance of winning and will surely find a solution. However, if you slump down, helpless, and avoid the fight even before you try, there will be no chance or hope of winning.

Then why do you need Taekwondo? As you learn Taekwondo skills through hard training, you naturally gain strength and dignity. There is one thing I always emphasize in my dojang: "You are stronger than you think!" Following the Master's instructions, you become used to doing things that you thought impossible at first. As you break seemingly unbreakable objects like thick boards or blocks, one by one, you gain the confidence that you can do whatever you put your mind to doing. As you pass difficult promotion tests, your belt level continues higher. You see your growth with your own eyes. Through this process, you gain a sense of challenge and achievement. That doubles your self-confidence in your capability and value. And the power of your confidence is naturally released from your strengthened inner-being. People around you will easily sense your powerful inner-strength.

This strength is first evident in the eyes. The eyes are the windows of the mind. Words may deceive but the eyes cannot. Your self-confidence radiates through your bright eyes. Second, it shows through your words. You gain a clear, confident voice and manner of speech. You become able to lead relationships with others. Third, it exudes from your body through an open chest, a straight posture, and a lively gait. People feel your healthy energy. They perceive you as a trustworthy person. Lastly, a full-face smile! He who laughs is strong. He who is not strong cannot laugh confidently. If you have such a confident look, people will treat you with respect.

"Here we go! Open your eyes wide, clear your throats, tighten your stomachs, spread open your chests, and kihap! Aah-!" At once, the look in the students' eyes change, and their attitude turns confident. I present them their new belts in front of their families. Their families are proud and the students are self-satisfied. The promotion tests wrap up like that.

When I first opened the dojang, all sorts of people came to quarrel, including neighboring black belts and instructors, village toughs, and people practicing other martial arts. Each time, rather than direct confrontation, I showed them I wasn't someone they could mess with. In most cases, they conceded and turned away. I always outwardly smiled and looked confident, but I held a knife in my heart, determined to fight to my death if it ever came to it. Later, as friends, they would tell me that they couldn't bring themselves to attack me because they sensed an unexpected chill. Empty words mean nothing, but when there is inner strength to back them up, words will work.

Win before the fight! I explain that this is the first purpose and reason to learn Taekwondo. Once you get entangled in a battle, you will suffer regardless of whether you win or lose. If you win before the match, you won't unnecessarily waste any energy, and sometimes you can find a friend in your enemy. Living your daily life, no matter how difficult, with confidence and diligence will help build up your powerful inner-strength. That, I emphasize, is Taekwondo training and Taekwondo strategy.

Mr. Tough Guy

A friend's father passed away. We decided to meet at another friend's house to comfort him. He had immediately flown back to Korea when he heard that his father was in a critical condition, but he had still been unable to make it in time. Those who have parents back in Korea all worry about being unfilial in the same way. Anyhow, feeling that even if I couldn't share happy occasions, I should at least be present to share the sad ones, I drove quickly after closing the dojang.

Around ten men were sitting around in a circle. A few of them were friends I had never met before. After a brief greeting, I sat with them. There were bottles of liquor rolling around, and the atmosphere was somehow tense, ugly. Loud voices were being exchanged. One man, whom I had never met before, seemed to be harshly provoking others. He was so fierce that no one could get him to stop.

Unable to suppress his anger any longer, another man grabbed a liquor bottle and tried to attack. I got up and grabbed his arm, and snatched away the bottle. Watching me step up and stop this man, the fierce friend started confronting me. "You're the Taekwondo Master?" He tried to provoke me, demanding me to 'fight him if I was so good.' What use is arguing with a drunken man? I replied calmly and tried to let it go. But he would not stop. He insisted that he had practiced mixed martial arts and boxing for 20 years and that he was still in good shape from weight training and exercise.

Moreover, everyone was giving me looks that said, 'Do something about him!' Thinking that the atmosphere would only get rougher if we stayed inside anyway, I suggested we go outside.

If a Taekwondo Master hits someone, it is attempted murder. If you fight, then you get into big trouble for using your fists. If you don't fight, then you become known as a Master who cannot even protect himself. I could not hit nor get hit. I had to resolve this situation while unable to go either direction.

The two of us stood opposite each other in a dark alley. Since the man said he had done mixed martial arts, I asked him if he knew how to do a low kick. He said he is good at it. I told him to kick me with his low kick. The man looked at me with an absurd expression and asked, "Really?" "Of course!" I gritted my teeth and stuck out my thigh. With an expression that said, 'You're so dead,' he kicked my thighs hard. There was a loud noise and my thighs hurt, but it was bearable. "Wow, you're really strong!" I complimented him and told him to kick me again. Truly angered, he kicked me on the same spot. There was another loud 'wham,' and it hurt so much. But I still stood and endured.

I smiled and asked if I could try kicking this time. Snorting, the man agreed. I stood with my guard up. I stepped forward, pulled back my waist and roundhouse kicked with my left foot.

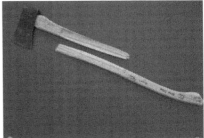

With a loud 'wham!' the man staggered and then collapsed. I quickly held him up before his knees hit the ground. However dislikeable he may be, to have the man on his knees would hurt his pride for the rest of his life. I slung him over my shoulders and said, "Hey, so it's true you've worked out. You're still standing even after my kick, that's amazing!" Unable to sit or stand, his mouth hung open speechlessly. He couldn't stand on his own; his legs had already given out. What would he do if I suddenly jumped at him? "What, is this not enough? Do you want to try punching too?" Fear rose in his wide eyes. He shook his head.

I waited for him to gather himself before suggesting we go back inside. Everyone stared at us with wide eyes as we entered the room. "what on earth was that sound?" "I don't know?" But everyone seemed to guess what had happened, seeing the sudden politeness in the man's attitude.

Afterward, I kept quiet in fear of embarrassing the man. But the incident didn't hush itself just because I kept my mouth shut. Later, the man unexpectedly visited our home. I had been worrying how I would face him after the terrible first impression, but he came up to me first. We apologized to each other and ended up laughing. After that, we all become friends with each other. He turned out to be a good friend. He was a talented man who worked as a middle-management engineer in a large company. Whenever his help was needed, he would drop even his own work and rush to help, to make up for that day's offense. He became a great friend to everyone.

After becoming close friends, people cackle with laughter when mentioning that day's incident. They tease, "Hey, if you're getting itchy, why don't you have a match with Master Lee?" I tell them, "Oh, stop it. It's in the past, and it's getting embarrassing." The friend good-naturedly replies, "Do you think I'm crazy? To do that again? I'm already having a hard time making up for it. At any rate, you guys would have all been dead that day if not for Master Lee, jeez!" And everyone ends up laughing at that.

Looking back, there's one thing I did right. Holding him when he collapsed. Trying to protect his last bit of pride, even if he was an opponent. If it weren't for that, I would have never had the chance to make such a good friend. Don't they say that men are enemies in fights but friends in company?

Madame X

Madame X gave off wrong impression from her very first visit to the dojang. She glared at people with her arms folded, and it was clear that she was not a friendly person. She was short, pudgy, and stiff, but she copied moves recklessly without following the proper steps. Even when asked to be careful, she was obstinate. She would then fall and twist her ankles. After a few weeks off, she would return and come at her partners aggressively. No one liked being her partner. Even when told that this was not a fistfight, she would not listen.

She always came to me before and after class to ask strange questions. "What do I do in a fight? When can I do the 540-degree tornado kick?" I could not keep acting nice either. "Madame X, hands high and feet low. Aim for the eye with your hand and the groin with your feet. Kick as fast as possible and run for your life. You cannot do a 540-degree tornado kick at your level, and even if you could, it doesn't always work in an actual situation," I scolded her. But even then, she continued to demand to learn some 'fighting techniques.'

A year later, Madame X came in smiling brightly and handed me the results of her medical check-up. She told me that before Taekwondo, every category was abnormal and she had so many medicines she had to take. This year, she had lost 20 pounds, and most of the test categories had turned back to normal. In short, her last year's test results were 'not dead, so alive,' while this year's test results were 'living healthily and energetically.' She highly complimented me, saying that this was also Master Lee's report card for the past year. Then she asked if she could have a private talk, so I set up a counseling appointment.

The next day, Madame X came in and abruptly told me how these days, she could park in front of her yard and walk to her porch alone. How satisfying that simple act was. Before that, she would call her husband, and he would have to accompany her from her car to their house. That was how she had lived for the last thirty years. There was a reason.

She told me she used to be very fit and popular when she was 17 years old. One night, she came back from her cheerleading practice, parked her car in front of the yard, and unlocked the front door, when she sensed someone behind her. She turned around and came face-to-face with something. Only much later, she realized it must have been a burly man's chest. She looked up and, with a flash of light, fell unconscious. When she later came to, she was on a hospital bed in the emergency room. Her father had found her lying naked in front of the porch, covered in blood and her clothes torn to pieces, her face bludgeoned unrecognizably. She had been assaulted and raped. They assumed that the suspect was someone living nearby, but were unable to catch the culprit.

After that, it was not just her violated body, but also her soul that was destroyed. She could not trust anyone, and that walk from the car to the front door was terrifying. She lived 30 years like that. How horrifying it is, to have such a big wound eat into one's soul and follow one around like shackles all those years. But after learning Taekwondo, as her health and physical strength returned, her confidence grew as well. Now she would think, 'If a bastard like that ever comes along again! This time he's going to die!' After changing her mind like that, she felt refreshed and happy with her life.

Hearing her story, I was speechless. It was my first time directly interacting with a rape victim and imagining the shock of the incident, I was ever so sorry and heartbroken. I regretted my dislike and narrow-mindedness towards her, ignorant of her circumstances. After that, I also changed my attitude. I tried to be as kind as I could and answered her questions with sincerity. As a result, Madame X has dramatically improved her skills. She is quite skilled with moves that are difficult for most adults. She has good power, and her stability has increased with better coordination. She is doing even better than my expectations. Time to time, I deliberately get hit, and her strength makes it very painful. Sometimes, her foot accidentally flies down below the belt, and I have to jump away in fright to avoid it. At those times, I think getting hit by that foot could make a cripple out of a man.

Her relationships with other students have also improved. She comfortably strikes up conversations first and smiles often. She used to have problems with relationships at work, but these days she's hearing comments of how she is doing much better.

Rather than Taekwondo, I think her newly found confidence and belief in herself were what saved Madame X from those hellish times. And wouldn't the fresh energy rising from a healthy body create that kind of confidence?

Wise Masters' teachings say training right and cleansing your energy will make the turbid energy retreat and the misfortune leave. It is the logic of bright light driving the darkness away. Just as a magnet draws in a magnet, fresh energy draws in fresh energy while dark energy attracts dark energy. What place is a prison? Is it not a place where people with dark energy gather? It is a place where birds of a feather flock together and suffer. Look around. Those who are happy get along better with others who are happy, while those who are unhappy often end up hanging around unhappy people. Therefore, if we fill ourselves with fresh energy and light up the dojang, all the problems surrounding our lives will soon disappear or, at least, seem manageable.

A modern-day dojang should become a charging station where you fill up with clear and bright energy through training your body and mind. And its Master should be the spring, the source of energy in that charging station. If we could see the dojang as an energy business that provided modern people with the fresh energy, they needed to live new and satisfying lives, it would no longer be an ancient business but one of the modern eras. In this case, money would naturally follow as a bonus. If we could dig from the dojang precious value that people need but cannot find, then that would be striking gold.

A Street Fighter

When I first opened my dojang, other martial arts black-belts, masters and even street thugs barged in, demanding to see my skills or have a fight. At first, I was taken aback, but after a few years, such people stopped coming. It was because of the rumor that circulated – that no one could defeat me.

After 16 years, I left the town and moved to a far-away state. As I opened my new dojang, I anticipated the territorial attitudes I would have to overcome.

Then one day in class, I saw a sturdy-looking man sitting at the back with his arms folded. Of course, I thought he was one of my students' family member, but he remained even after class had ended. When I asked how I could help him, he immediately hurled insults at me with a scowl. "Everything you do here is b***s***. Martial arts are all b***s*** and so are you. I've come to put an end to all this fake lark." And then he said, "I'm a professional street fighter. I can finish the likes of you in a single blow, let's fight!"

I was not exactly new to such displays, but even in my experience, few people were this blatant in picking a fight. His expression told me that he was impatient to strike a punch on my face in that moment. Looking at his stiff neck, his thick arms and legs, and his eyes burning with conceit, he was not an easy man to deal with. From my experience, such men do not back off with words. Even if I send him away, he would return puffed up to cause bigger problems. I had to dissuade him somehow.

I sat him down, offering to hear what the problem was and why he wanted to fight. When I asked him what he did, he answered that he was a professional fighter. He said that people like him did street fighting among themselves, and every win earned him $100. That he wears a 16-ounce glove and beats his opponent until they surrender.

I felt a fire raging within, but painfully contained myself and politely asked, "Do you think you are a pro?" Of course, he was a pro. "Then, did you do some research on me before coming?" At that, he glared at me and raised his voice. He told me that he didn't care, that I should stop changing the subject and decide whether I was going to face him or not. I pressed down the surge of anger and asked one more question. "You do street fighting for fun, don't you?" He said he did.

I jumped up and punched down onto my desk. Of all things, my keyboard was in the spot where my fist came down. The keyboard smashed into pieces and spattered in all directions like popcorn. A handful of pieces flew towards the man's face and he recoiled back in astonishment. His eyes widened at the sudden change in my attitude. "Hey! I don't fight for fun when I fight!" I shouted like a thunderclap.

I raised my fist, bleeding from the broken keyboard pieces, as if to nail it onto his head and continued. "I don't fight for fun! I fight to death! If you were thinking of fighting me, you should have come with the resolve to either live or die. Yet someone who fights for fun dares to challenge to me?" He must have seen me as an easy target since I was teaching children and wanted to have some fun and make some gossip by beating me up. "You don't even know what a real fight is, I don't wear gloves when I fight! Do you think you are tough? You chose the wrong person today! You go around picking fights without knowing how wide the world is!" He wore a frightened expression at my raving energy.

Probably thinking this was not a good idea after all, he stood up and tried to leave. I burst out, "Where are you going? Sit back down!" The man hesitantly sat down again. "You think you are a pro, don't you? Hey! A real pro doesn't fight for $100! Does that get you anything more than pain relief pads? And are you messing around knowing the state law?" He asked me what that was. To do boxing or MMA fighting, you must apply for an athlete registration and with it, attach a general physical examination and a certified document of a head CT scan stating you have no brain damage. Furthermore, if you are to earn money from the bout, you must register with the state government's Sports Competition Committee. State law also requires the competition to be carried out under the supervision of a coach, a referee, and a doctor, who are all issued certificates, and each competition must be paid and authorized. Attack skills other than those permitted by the state's Sports Competition Committee cannot be used.

I demanded how he calls himself a professional without even knowing what is legal and what is illegal, and he said the local policemen pay to watch. I added, "Are the policemen the law? They just threw you a few bucks and enjoyed watching you fight like an animal. You play the fool like that, yet recklessly pick a fight, having no previous research on your opponent nor any strategy? You're what they call an amateur!" I then kept pushing him into a corner with words. "A lot of tough guys like you were crushed by me. I usually don't get this angry, but you immediately started this conversation with insults and your ignorant and poor attitude. If I didn't put up with it, you would have already been crushed!" The mettlesome, large man suddenly shrank like a student told off by the principal.

I asked him if street fighting was his job, and he answered no. That he has another job, and the fighting is for fun. "Right? This is my job and my life's everything. I bet my whole life on this, and I've come all the way here, breaking every joint of my body. And yet an amateur like you who is not even on the same level challenges me!"

"If I fight you, and by some chance, I lose, I have to close down my dojang from embarrassment. Even if I win, who would trust their children with someone who fights with local thugs? Either way, as soon as I fight with you, my reputation will crack, my dojang will close, and my life may be ruined. Yet do you think I will send you away after just a few punches?

Commonly in martial arts strategies, they teach us to abandon our flesh and break the opponent's bones, to abandon our bones and give the opponent his quietus. But I go further than that. Once I get into a fight,

I am someone who throws away the idea of living and fights with the resolve to die. I do not fight to win, nor do I fight to live. I just fight to death. One who fights for fun cannot beat someone who fights to win, and one who fights to win cannot overcome someone who fights to die.

"If I do get in a fight, I have no intention of keeping you alive. I will die with you. So, if you are prepared to die, go for it!" Afraid that the situation was not going the way he expected, the man told me he just fights for fun and had no intention of risking his life, and that he understood what I said. He left rapidly as if escaping.

After he left, I picked up the scattered pieces of the broken keyboard and saw my bleeding hand. I felt pathetic. 'Ah, I still have a long way to go....'

I hate fighting. When I was young and recklessly fought against the thugs on the streets, I had nothing to lose. In my immaturity, I was even proud of my victories, despite being covered with blood. At the time, I was simple and ignorant. But now, there is too much more to lose than to gain. And I hate losing my mind and becoming a completely different person when I fight. So, unless it is a fight worth risking my life, I want to avoid fighting until the end. It is my wish to put those years of being 'Young and Wild' behind me and pass onto being 'Old and Wise'.

International Taekwondo Instructors, Who Are We?

We are Taekwondo Masters. We are not just leaders that teach the way of the martial arts; we are proud diplomats that plant the Korean spirit around the world. The Taekwondo rooted in the world today is the joint work of the dedicated instructors in Korea and the instructors who have left our homeland to plant the seeds of Korea with our blood and sweat.

Everyone agrees that the process of establishing a new life in an unfamiliar country is not easy. In the near future, we can laugh and talk about our hardships as fond memories, but if we were asked to do it all over again, we would shake our heads.

Twenty-three years ago, I entered American society and began finding my way. In this humble life, I have experienced many small and big things. I thought the United States was a place that I could survive only by fighting and winning. As a result, I have sustained many injuries already at this not-so-old age. They are wounds I received from acting rash to make up for my feelings of inferiority, from incidents that occurred because I couldn't be flexible, couldn't give in. I only realized later, that not making enemies, instead approaching people with a smile and making friends with love, is the best form of self-defense.

Chapter 5. Between Myth and Legend

Levitation

I met an eccentric man during my passionate youth. His hair was disheveled and his appearance shabby, but he was very learned in many areas. He dug soil during farming seasons, and then roamed around the world in leisure seasons. In any case, he didn't seem to be one to talk nonsense.

As our conversation deepened into the night, he suddenly said, "I'll ask you since you say you practice martial arts; have you heard of levitation? I couldn't believe it even after seeing it." One of his best friends learned Danjeon (human's energy field) breathing from his grandfather since childhood, and one day told the man that he'd show him levitation. The friend sat in meditation, slowly rose in the air and floated above the man's head before descending on the other side. How do you interpret this?

One of my senior Masters devoted his entire life to Chinese martial arts and Taekwondo training. It was (What was?) when he was sitting in a mountain cave, meditating with another person. Suddenly, the seat next to him felt empty, so he opened his eyes to see the other person floating above his head. He looked up for a long time and said, "Well, you're floating in the air." The person replied, "Am I?" and slowly came down. That person said he felt like he was floating but didn't realize he was really levitating.

It is said that Korean Buddhist monk Seung-sahn, known as one of the world's four living Buddha, also floated Yale students in the air in order to enlighten those who were suspicious of Buddha's teaching. He once explained the levitation. "It is merely a phenomenon in which the ground is full of positive energy, so if I fill my body with positive energy, they will just push each other away like a magnet with the same polarity."

Grand Master Woohyul and Tea Cup

There is a Grandmaster named Woohyul who taught me inner energy-training. Even at the age of eighty, he was well-built and maintained a level of speed, power, and flexibility in his kicks that a young man in his twenties could not possibly keep up with.

Once, after a long training, he poured me a freshly brewed cup of tea in an elegant teacup. I lifted the cup but quickly put it down from the heat. Nevertheless, my teacher effortlessly took his cup and slowly drank the tea. "Why do you not drink?" "It's too hot, Sir." At that, he asked me. "You still do not know how to send the energy in your hand and push out the heat of the teacup, do you?"

It happened that grandmaster Woohyul visited a fitness center when he was in the United States. Muscular men who were exercising with heavy weights watched an elderly Asian man, whose white beard came down to his chest, approach an American man and ask him to hold up as many weights as he could push on his legs, three times. When the American man lifted fifty in total out of the three times, grandmaster Woohyul sat on that very spot and lifted a hundred at once. Everyone's eyes went wide with surprise. Grandmaster Woohyul used to arm wrestle with his disciples only using his little finger, but no one has ever won against him.

I once asked my teacher about the late Zen master Chung-san, who was famous for showing a lot of extraordinary abilities. "Do you know mater Chung-san?" His answer was interesting. "Chung-san? I know him very well, he lived my next door!"

He continued, During the times of military government when Chung-san was most active, he was forcefully arrested by the infamous Central Intelligence Agency as he became socially influential. He was arrested without any charge, handcuffed, and haphazardly interrogated. "Do you really have that much power? If you do, show it to me now!" When the interrogator tried to browbeat, it was said Grandmaster Chung-san snapped off his handcuffs on the spot.

Quick Pace

My late maternal grandfather grew up as a woodcutter on Mountain Baekdu. (It is the highest mountain of Korea. Koreans assign a mythical quality to the volcano and its caldera lake, considering it to be their country's spiritual home.) It is said he even rode on the back of a tiger. I asked him how that was possible, and he replied that a tiger is a mystical creature and does not hurt people thoughtlessly.

Once, I climbed the mountain with my grandfather, who was over eighty-five years old at the time. As a young man of twenty, I ran ahead up the mountain path.

My grandfather followed me in mincing steps with a cane, his back bent to ninety degrees due to a lifetime of hard labor. At first, I outpaced him. Yet after a while, without a single puff, he breezed past me, who was breathing heavily. Afterwards, however hard I tried, I could not catch up with my grandfather. He glided up as if he was on an escalator, and it almost looked as if someone on the top of the mountain was pulling him up with an invisible rope.

He would climb up and wait for me to catch up. When I arrived, huffing and puffing, he would stand and continue up. He had to wait for me several times before we reached the summit. On the even ground, I did not notice but in the mountains, I just could not match my grandfather's pace. In those times, he would seem just like Yoda in the Star Wars movies, from his appearances to his way of speaking.

He was famous for his Quick Pace. When heading for a distant city to go to the market, he shocked people because he would catch up in half a day to other Mountain Baekdu woodcutters who left two days earlier. During the Japanese Occupation, he crossed the snowy Manchurian fields on foot between China and Russia to sell silk.

Even in his mid-eighties, my grandfather left home every morning with his bent back, relying on his cane and holding a hoe. He would come back after sunset with a cabbage or a white radish in hand. When I asked him where he had been, he would say he had gone to take care of the vegetable garden he had left in his old neighborhood. The problem was that the place was not at a distance that even I, a young man in his twenties, could dare to walk in a day. I couldn't believe that an old man walked that distance on a cane and labored, without even riding a car. My grandfather always went through the mountains when heading somewhere far. He told me that when looking at a mountain, he could see that mountain's pulse, and walking by the pulse enabled him to walk quickly and easily.

Furthermore, when he took a taxi in the middle of the busy Seoul, he would teach the driver directions in an old Hamgyeong-do dialect seen in a historical drama. "You can't go this way, Mr. driver. The road is blocked!" "Don't worry, sir, I know the way." Yet indeed, the road would be blocked from constructions or accidents. When a driver asked him how he knew, the answer was, "I just know!" I am guessing that he gained special insight and learned how to read the geographical features from climbing mountains and crossing fields for a long time.

Palm Blast

A senior Master who had lived his life training in martial arts happened to see an elderly monk's Palm Blast. He recklessly followed the monk into the mountains, leaving the world behind. The little temple where the elderly monk, well known to be a spiritually enlightened Buddhist priest, resided was located at South Korea's highest altitude and dates back to the Three Kingdom Period. Therefore, it is a very valuable cultural heritage. Yet even so, just as in the everyday world, frictions and struggles to occupy this place occurred frequently.

One day, a thug monk came, hired by those who wish to take possession of the temple. He obstinately picked a fight, claiming that if he won in a one-on-one fight with the old monk, he would take over the temple. Yet no matter what he said, the elderly monk paid him no heed. So, the thug went down to the town below the mountain, drank alcohol in daylight, danced naked and shouted, "I'm a monk from that temple!" Angry villagers visited the temple and protested, forcing the elderly monk to call in the thug monk.

"Very well, I shall fight you as you say. If you are defeated, you will train under me for a year, no exceptions!" And under that condition, the two men stood face to face in the temple yard. The thug had a metal flute tied to his arm under his sleeves, and this was his weapon. He was an owner of a deadly technique. When he speared a pine tree with its end, the flute would be nailed in inch deep at the height of one's philtrum, solar plexus, and groin. There were no few people who had been hurt by his flute.

As the thug monk whipped out his flute and posed for an attack, the elderly monk put his index finger and middle finger together, forced his hand forward, and the flute flew off the thug's hand. It was the Palm Blast. The old monk asked, "Do you admit defeat?", but the thug monk had already heard many things beforehand. Instead of being surprised, he stubbornly insisted, "Who lost? I only dropped my flute, I haven't even begun yet."

And so, this time the elderly monk put up his palm and shot a Palm Blast, and the thug monk who was about to pounce fell onto the ground. "Do you admit defeat?" Yet again, he insisted, "I just slipped on my own. I won't acknowledge it!" Angered, the elderly monk shot another Palm Blast. "Someone like him must be disciplined." The thug monk fell, coughing blood out of his mouth, with a shout. "Urk!"

Much later, the thug monk who returned to consciousness fell on his knees and begged for forgiveness. But it was too late. Afterward, he sat together with the senior Master, trapped in the temple, and trained reluctantly for a whole year.

Walk into the air

The elderly monk was left at the temple at a young age. His grandfather was a master of Taek-kyeon (traditional style of Taekwondo) and would sometimes visit the temple to teach him Taek-kyeon. However, feeling abandoned without parents in his young mind, the monk resisted against learning martial arts. And each time, his grandfather would rap his head with a long smoking pipe. Thus, he only reluctantly learned until "Three Stars Jumping step".

The Three Stars Jumping Step is a technique of remaining in the air, in which you jump and take three steps into the air and kick your opponent. Here, the three steps are not simple jumping steps but a mean to change directions in the air.

In the late period of Joseon dynasty, patriots who feared the world would be overthrown by foreign forces were caught in a secret meeting at a private residence and were surrounded by the royal forces. When the chief ordered them to surrender, these people burst out of the door and ran into all directions. Among them, one flew into the air and kicked the chief in his face and off his horse and rode the horse away. The rest of the people also escaped the siege like lightning and in the end, none of them were arrested. The technique used at this time was also the Three Stars Jumping Step. However, the Three Stars Jumping Step is not the highest move of Taek-kyeon; the best is the 'Seven Stars Jumping Step,' a level that his grandfather had mastered.

The senior Master is someone who trained in martial arts all his life, and of course was interested in learning. When he asked how long it would take to learn the Three Stars Jumping Step, the answer was that since he had trained sincerely for the past 3 years, it would only take another 3 years. However, the senior Master had come into the mountains leaving his wife and young daughter behind for 3 years and had already received the final divorce notification. He said that after the all the harsh training he had gone through, he did not think he could continue for another 3 years.

One Finger Stand

In the Shaolin Martial Arts, there is a technique called One Finger Stand. You gather energy at the tip of one finger and do a finger-stand. It requires so much energy in the finger that it could break through flesh and tear muscles. The senior Master asked the elderly monk, "Are you able to do the One Finger Stand?" "Of course!" was his answer.

"Eh, how can someone stand on one finger?" The monk said, "You say?", got up and hand-stood there with one hand on the floor. Then with a kihap, "I-yah!" he flicked the floor with his palm to stand just with the tip of his index finger. The senior Master could not close his mouth seeing this. The elderly monk said, "Did you see?" and sat back down.

Power of Thought

A disciple broke the elderly monk's prohibition and drank alcohol; he even took a nap afterwards. He was caught, but afraid of punishment, he lied that he had not drunk alcohol. The old monk bellowed, "How dare you try to fool your master, must you break your skull to wake up?" Blue lights flashed in his eyes. "Bang! Bang! bang!" The disciple suddenly banged his head against the ground and fainted. Later, when the senior Master asked him what happened, the disciple said that it felt like someone had grabbed the back of his head and banged it against the ground. Even though he felt like his head was going to split, there was nothing he could do.

One day, the elderly monk asked the senior Master. "Why do you martial artists fight to bleed? It is messy." "What? Then how do you fight, sir?" The answer was unexpected. "You could get ahold of the opponent's breath below his nose!" It was a method of getting ahold of another's breath to prevent air going through the nose. When suddenly suffocated, even the most powerful man falls and faints. Such techniques are called the Power of Thoughts. It is a way of dealing with one's opponent only using the power of the mind.

The Power of Tai Chi

Before China opened up like today, a martial arts group from Taiwan visited mainland China. They asked the Communist Party to see the Chen family style Tai Chi in particular. The Communist Party found the eldest son of Chen, a family known for its traditional Tai Chi, and ordered him to demonstrate. However, the eldest son was already an old man working on a wheat farm. He refused, saying that his parents and grandfathers were all killed during the revolution and that he learned nothing about Tai Chi.

However, in face of headstrong insistence and the promise of 'just once', he demonstrated. The Taiwanese martial artists dared not say anything in face of what they saw.

A Korean martial artist heard this news and became so curious that he recklessly flew to China and asked the son to show him a single demonstration. The eldest son replied with "No, I don't know," but he became tired after a month of begging. The martial artist promised, "I'll go back to Korea after one demonstration!" In the middle of the night, the eldest son called out the martial artist to the side street of the hotel that he was staying at. Standing in the dark alley, he hit the hotel wall with his palm and the entire hotel building shook. He then told the speechless man to go back now that he had seen it and disappeared. This was the Tai Chi's secret technique which we had only heard in stories.

Flying Sword

A good-natured senior Master whom I met in the United States had been absorbed in traditional martial arts, Inner energy training from a very young age. From a certain moment, he was able to learn some Taoist magic. He could read other people's minds or intentionally manipulate their thoughts and even received clairvoyant powers that allowed him to see things from afar.

Many people sought him out, impressed by these amazing superpowers, but these powers were not always helpful. If a person with an ill liver came near, he would feel unbearable pain in his own liver, and if someone with a bad kidney came near, he would suffer from the pain in his own kidney. So, everyone would be surprised when he asked them, "Your liver is unwell, is it not? You have a problem with your kidney, do you not?" He read others' energies with his body.

Out of all his skills, I was most interested in "Flying Sword". It is a technique of throwing swords into the air through telekinesis. One day, a man who had heard of his talents paid him a visit. He told the Master to stop lying and to demonstrate his skills if he indeed possessed them.

"Are you confident that you will not regret it?" The man only snorted. Suddenly, the sword hanging on the wall slipped out of its sheath and flew across the air and under the man's neck. The sharp sword was hanging in the air, right under his throat. The man turned deathly pale and one could see his hair sticking up. "I could cut your throat without even leaving a fingerprint. Do you still doubt me?"

With such abilities, what would there be to fear? However, his actual situation seems to have been different. The more psychic power he had, the more pain he felt and the more volatile his personality became. People around him avoided him because of the murderous energy that spread out from him. Time to time, he would lose control and become violent, to the point that he feared that he might kill someone someday. Eventually, this toxic energy even affected his family, and after suffering untellable hardships, he gave up all his powers and left Korea.

Those super powers are a phenomenon in which a third-party energy enters our mind and exerts superhuman abilities. There is nothing free in the world. After drawing special energy and using it, we must pay as much. However, if continued, you become crushed by the energy and your body and spirit are destroyed. That is why truth-seekers are sternly told not to even glance at the temptation of super power that they encounter through their journey towards the truth.

I studied Physics and wrote a book <The Science of Taekwondo>. Yet, what I had really been interested in since my childhood was the mysterious martial arts tale. The stories I described up will be interesting to some and sound hollow to others. However, looking at the martial art skills and sincerity of those who tell such stories, I was convinced that these were not necessarily exaggerated or fictional.

Truthfully, it is said that everything within human imagination can happen in this universe. Quantum mechanics and theory of relativity teach us that probability is so low that it is difficult to see with our own eyes, but this does not mean impossibility. Is it not said that things that seem impossible, such as teleportation of objects, are theoretically possible but just not yet within our current technology? So, if you asked me whether if these things are real or not, I would like to vote that they do exist.

But there is a fun anecdote. Two monks made their way into the mountains to train for twenty years, away from the world. After twenty years of asceticism, they left the mountain and came across a river. One monk walked on top of the water across the river, and the other paid two cents to cross the river on a boat. The boatman asked, "That monk walks across the water, what did you do for twenty years to cross water on this boat?" The monk replied, "That man has spent twenty years training only to save two cents. In that time, I have learned the eternal truth of the universe." In other words, do not waste time on things that have little use.

Epilogue

Summer of rain showers, autumn of blue skies, winter of frost, and spring that returned once again… Looking back, all the people, friends, and students who have come through my life have been precious to me. Setting down my restless mind that only looked to tomorrow, I found that no time had not been valuable and no incident had not been beautiful. At every moment of my life, all meetings were meant to be, and all episodes had something to teach. The place I stood was the very corner of paradise.

My childhood dream was to become an international Taekwondo instructor. That was the extent of my dream, and it came true. I no longer had a goal to wish for nor a place to go. I suddenly felt lost. Where should I go now, for what? I regret that I did not live more wisely. Whether I like it or not, it is time to pull myself once again together to go forth in my life. It is time to step up, dreaming new dreams.

I wish to be a Master who does not become rusty with time, a warrior who wins without fighting. I wish to live a transparent life, brushing away the dust of the soul, as an ascetic that reaches virtue (*do*) with my hands and feet (*taekwon*). And one day, when I complete my mission given by heaven and leave this world, I wish to leave wearing my uniform, my lifetime partner, as a shroud. Until that day, I want to go slowly but always surely forward, feeling the gentle wind on my face.